RECLAIMING
HAPPINESS

RECLAIMING HAPPINESS

8 Strategies for an Authentic Life and Greater Peace

Nicola Phoenix
MSc, BSc, CP.AMT, DipFryog

FINDHORN PRESS

Published in 2011 by Findhorn Press, Scotland

ISBN 978-1-84409-542-1

Edited by Lizzie Hutchins
Cover design by Richard Crookes
Interior design by Damian Keenan
Printed and bound in in the European Union

1 2 3 4 5 6 7 8 9 17 16 15 14 13 12 11

Published by
Findhorn Press
117-121 High Street,
Forres IV36 1AB,
Scotland, UK

t +44 (0)1309 690582
f +44 (0)131 777 2711
e info@findhornpress.com
www.findhornpress.com

Contents

Acknowledgements

This book is written with gratitude and appreciation for the many people who have helped, supported, cared for, loved and encouraged me and paved the way for my own growth with their teachings. You may not have realized just how important you were or are to me and I may not have been able to express it at the time, but right now is all I have, so thank you.

To my students, clients and everyone I have worked with, helped and supported so far, thank you for also being my teachers in life. I am a better person for having met every single one of you. I hope that you are able to learn to see the magnificence that I see in each and every one of you.

Special thanks and love go to the wonderful Findhorn Press family: my editor Lizzie, Sue Blake and to the many people who help me to help others.

And to my parents and family,

but most of all to Hayden,

thank you.

Introduction

Give up thinking of others.
If you want to think of others,
think of your own Self in them.
Give up looking at others.
If you want to look at others,
look at your own Self in them.
Look at your own Self,
and become immersed in your own ecstasy.
—SWAMI MUTKANANDA

If we thought of others in a new way, without our habitual judgements, would we see something different in them? Would we see more deeply into who they were? Would we even see their spark of magnificence and limitless potential?

This is an intriguing idea, but what about seeing ourselves in that way too? We usually make far too many negative assumptions about ourselves to manage this. Seeing ourselves as magnificent is just a joke. Experiencing true happiness seems an unattainable dream. But what if things could change?

Let's brainstorm for a moment. What do you think you'd need in order to experience real happiness — presuming, of course, you aren't experiencing it right now? I'm not talking about what you'd have to own or even achieve; I'm talking about *you*. How would *you* need to be different?

You may feel as though you don't know the answer right now. You may just be feeling that something is lacking, that things could be better, that you're lost, in pain, alone, that life is just happening to you rather than you truly living it. But it's precisely in those moments that you can reclaim happiness — happiness that has been hidden away for far too long!

LOOKING OUT OR IN?

The external world has a huge impact on many of us, and looking out at that world is the direction we've chosen for our life and success. So we follow fashion or what society advocates — but then what are we left with? The feeling that it has all been a waste of time and money? Disappointment because yet another fad has failed to give us what we needed? In short, a lack of long-term fulfilment?

If we focus too much on developments outside ourselves, whatever they are, we'll miss the opportunities to develop within. So think for a moment — are you working to achieve inner peace or to buy the next digital thingamajig? Which is more important?

Ultimately, the external things that we're trying so desperately to obtain are only transitory. A new fashion will come along soon — something faster, more compact, in a new colour or style. Progress is great and I'm all for it, but there's a lot more to life than that.

Society's over-consumption at least shows us that having more doesn't make us happy. Maybe we needed to get to this place of over-consumption and waste to realize that we already had the most important thing there was: ourselves!

In the grand scheme of things, we are actually all we've got, but so often we put restrictions on our happiness and the inward journey to reclaim this. I know because I've done it myself. I spent many years being extremely unhappy. I built a set of negative patterns around myself that reinforced my unhappiness. So what changed? I realized that misery didn't make me happy — hardly rocket science — and that in order to get rid of it I had to find out why I wasn't happy.

We're all different in how we go about recognizing that it's time to change. Some of us choose the gradual route of learning and growing, while others, like me, opt for a lengthy period of pain, 'dis-ease' and suffering which gives us a good kick up the backside! Whatever your story, right here and now is where you will change. You've already decided to, I know — that's why you're reading this book!

CHOOSING TO BE HAPPY

I believe that if we choose to, we can all be happy. I believe that we're put here to experience happiness, health, nourishment, fulfilment and a divine connection with everyone and everything — it's our birthright. But I've met far too many people who aren't embracing a life that will make them truly happy — and that's not just because I'm a psychologist! Take a look for yourself. How many people around you are really happy? In fact, take a look at the lengths that some people will go to *distract themselves* from embracing a natural state of happiness.

More to the point, if you're not happy yourself, what can you do about it? The answer is simple: you can learn how to make yourself happy. That's what you want, after all, isn't it?

THE LIGHTBULB MOMENT

I was brought up in a family that believed strongly that there was a solution to every problem. When it came to health, nature had the answers, so I looked to nature and learned about it. What was my part in the big scheme of things? I looked at that question on every level, from the physical to the metaphysical to the scientific, and within both Eastern and Western philosophies. I dedicated this stage of my life to discovering how the universe worked and how I played a part in that. However, I found out that the most important thing was not just to read about things but to actually experience them — to incorporate the principles into my life.

So, when I became disillusioned with my life, I thought I needed to dramatically change myself — become lovable, healthy and a better person — before happiness would arrive. But I eventually realized that the only reason I couldn't find happiness was because I thought that something was missing from myself. Nothing *was* missing — I was already all there. I just didn't know what I was looking for or how to find it. Then I had a lightbulb moment as all of the points of my learning led me to see:

We are all right now and in every way totally complete.

Yes, we are! You may think this is crazy, because you'll never *really* be complete until you've lost weight, got a job, built a solid relationship, bought a house, succeeded in your career, made yourself look different, become completely healthy, to mention but a few. How many times have you said: 'I'd be happy if…'? Even in our everyday speech we often place restrictions on achieving happiness. But why limit yourself?

The point is, are you going to remain unhappy until you've achieved your goals (and they may not bring you real happiness anyway) or are you going to learn to embrace your magnificence right now? Which would you rather do?

THE CHOICE TO GO FORWARD

By reading this book, you're choosing to go forward. That will involve making a journey within — to discover real joy and happiness rather than relying on transitory external stimuli to provide it. I remember how, as a teenager, I first learned to turn my mind inward through yoga techniques and meditation. It was as if I'd discovered a new dimension — and I literally had! However, as often happens when we're introduced to the tools that can help us, I didn't fully devote myself to these practices until years later, after I'd endured a lot more pain and despair.

Eastern philosophy pointed me towards a deeper understanding of my being, and no matter how hard I tried to avoid acknowledging those ideas, I knew they were correct. As I gradually came to a major point of change, I allowed myself to find out more. In classical texts, I read over and over again that we are all part of the divine. This was such a new concept for me. So I indulged myself in some new thinking, and most of all new experiencing, and the outcome was incredible.

In this book, I'll teach you what I learned. I'll give you the tools to embrace the magnificence you are right now and experience the happiness that brings. I'm not suggesting that this is the only path to change. But I know from experience that it can work.

This journey of personal transformation does involve taking action. And I do really mean now — yes, even today! The past is over and the future hasn't happened yet, so why do we let them rule our lives? Is it because the past wasn't what we wanted it to be (or maybe it was so good, nothing could ever be that good again)? Is it because the future might not live up to our expectations? Believe me, with a few changes, it probably will. Either way, the present moment is all we have to make the most of this precious opportunity that is on our doorstep.

I discovered that the only way to change was to go within and address my own traumas, experiences, beliefs and actions, and I continue to do this. I don't mean that I continually review my past or engage in eternal questioning — I just live my life, and if fear or limited beliefs hold me back, I address them, change them and move on in a new way, as you'll see from the examples throughout this book.

Realizing that I could change the way I was thinking, feeling and behaving began to affect my environment, my mood and even my immune system in subtle ways. As a result, I got well, became happier and, most importantly, began to help others, which to me is the greatest gift of all.

Inevitably, along the way, I've met people who have tested and challenged me. Looking back, I'm grateful to each and every one of them for everything they've taught me. I can honestly say that I now feel only love for them. I've had an amazing journey, moving through anger and disappointment to forgiveness, love and peace. All of these experiences have been catalysts for so much growth and change. It becomes impossible to see them as bad when great learning, growth and ultimately peace have come from them.

Why hold on to old hurts when they prevent us from feeling happy? And so often we not only cling to them but also allow ourselves to project them onto new situations and people. Think of all the negative judgements that you've made about brand new and trouble-free situations — judgements based purely on your past experiences.

YOU'RE THE SAME AS ME!

These may not be the only judgements you're making without really questioning yourself. Many of us think that people with more money, bigger houses or better jobs are better off than we are. In fact, we may even think that they're better human beings than we are. But I've worked with global business leaders and well-known personalities, and I can tell you that 'having it all' doesn't make any difference to their tendency towards self-loathing and insecurity. I'm not suggesting that successful people aren't happy, because quite a few of them are extremely happy. However, I'd like to dispel the illusion that it's always easier for those who are 'better off' to be happy than it is for you. We all have the potential. After all, we all are the same.

We're not even separate from each other. We may look and sound totally different, as may our rituals and behaviour. But strip away these external differences and you'll see that we're all here to learn, grow and experience life.

Taking this deeper, we all — yes, every single one of us — originate from the same divine source. This concept of oneness is paramount in learning how to create a life of peace and happiness.

DOING IT FOR OURSELVES

So, if we're all capable of being happy, let's now consider what 'personal success' really is. Contrary to many people, I view this as being very different from the mere accumulation of material possessions. To my way of thinking, personal success is reclaiming our power to go within and rediscover the connection with our own true self. This inner journey allows us to create a happy peaceful being whose outer life is subsequently full of joy.

It's the difference between taking a fairground ride and riding a bicycle: we either sit and let life take us round and round a familiar route or we use our own mode of transportation and start heading towards where we want to go. And by empowering ourselves, we can attract anything into our life, including the abundance, love and peace we wish for.

I'm suggesting that we can do this from a place of happiness rather than putting up with unhappiness until we have achieved the goal(s) that we believe will bring us happiness. This place of happiness is the inner self. I call it the 'real self'. Why? 'Real' to me means that we already are all we are and ever will be, but it isn't limiting — it doesn't mean we can't move forward and experience much more.

Most of us have become disconnected from this real self, and in this book we're going to look at the reasons why. These are misunderstandings rather than immovable blockages. In this book we'll be working through misunderstandings about:

1. our *true divine nature*
2. our *personal power*
3. our *safety, stability and illusions*
4. our *possessions, desires and ownership*
5. our *anger, resentment and blame*
6. our *self-love*
7. our *pathway to inner peace and harmony*
8. our *personal fulfilment.*

These are old patterns we need to be *diverted away from*. Imagine walking down a road and seeing a puddle. Instead of getting your feet wet, you make a conscious decision to navigate around it. That is a diversion. In this book, you'll be diverting away from unhealthy thoughts and behaviour and taking a new route through life.

This doesn't have to be a lengthy, complicated, expensive upheaval. I'm not suggesting that to avoid getting your feet wet you need to get a pilot's licence, save up for a plane and fly over the puddle. If you're willing to change, you're already halfway there. Each chapter will suggest a diversion we can take to get round a misunderstanding:

1. a diversion away from *separation*
2. a diversion away from *the influence of others*
3. a diversion away from *fear*
4. a diversion away from *attachment*
5. a diversion away from *pain*
6. a diversion away from *resistance*
7. a diversion away from *disorder*
8. a diversion away from *dissatisfaction.*

I've also included simple exercises and techniques to help you. Some of these involve methods of breathing and relaxing to calm anxiety, while others provide visualizations to keep you feeling grounded and peaceful within. I can't emphasize enough the importance of practising these techniques rather than just reading through them; change won't happen unless we actually change ourselves!

Throughout the book, I will also often ask you questions. I recommend that you give the same attention to these as you give to the exercises. Don't simply read them, but stop and answer them. Write the answers down or note them mentally.

They aren't intended to judge you in any way, but to help you look at things differently.

Don't think that these techniques and exercises will consume your already busy life or be yet another pressure on top of everything else. They are intended to support you while you try to create something better. You can also begin to build up your own toolkit of techniques, starting with these and incorporating others that life brings you along the way. Don't just use them every now and then — remember that this toolkit is for life. When you're stressed, there will be a tool to help you regain a sense of calm. When you catch yourself thinking negative or fearful thoughts, there will be a way out of the cycle. When you are crying out in despair, there will be a friendly voice that once cried out too, but is now showing you that anything is possible.

This journey that we will be taking together will lead you to embrace all that you are and experience the happiness that you want. It's really that simple — though of course, like life itself, it's what you put in that shapes it.

So let's take the first steps together...

Chapter 1

Misunderstanding our True Divine Nature:
Diverting Away from Separation

It is ignorance of our real nature that causes the Self to be obscured. When ignorance is destroyed, the Self is liberated from its identification with the world. This liberation is Enlightenment.

— PATANJALI

You are reading this because you want to change. I am writing this because I am in the process of changing.

You may have expected me to say that I have changed and am now completely connected in every way possible and walking around in a continual state of bliss. I am not. If I had said I was, that would have been my ego stepping in and letting you think that we are different or that I am better than you. But we aren't different — that is the whole point. You, me, your neighbour, my friends — we are all the same. I may have learned and remembered a few things at a different time from you, but that's not because we are different but because our paths in life have been different until now.

We cannot measure our own journey against another person's — we're all individuals and every step of our journey has been important. There hasn't been a moment of wasted time, for each step has brought us closer to where we are now.

THE 'I' AND 'WE'

We all have different parents, live in different places and have been brought up with different ideas about life. Yet we can all learn from them and move forward. The limiting factor for us all is our thoughts and *beliefs*, not our *situation*.

I have studied with many great teachers and at first I often put them on a pedestal. I didn't think that I was as good as they were. They were teaching me, however, that we were all the same. It was my insecurities that were the blocks to seeing that spark of divine nature within us all.

I also spent many years believing that I wasn't good enough because I was dyslexic. I let other people's comments crush any belief in my writing ability. I let my interpretation of the situation hold me back, not the situation itself. And here you are now, reading my words in a bestselling book.

Do you think you aren't good enough in some way? Or that you aren't valuable? Think for a moment about how your role — your job, your life, your gifts — fits into making the world work, making it a better place. Take the time right now to see how you bring benefit to others. I have had many clients who have answered that they bring no benefit at all! You may be thinking this too, but you are part of humanity and you do bring a particular quality to the world.

You may be thinking that you will be good enough or worthy when you are different — when you have that successful business, that new career, that new home… We often feel we need outer success to prove ourselves to others. But why do we have to prove ourselves? Why does it even matter what other people think of us? Welcome to the misunderstanding of our true divine nature.

SEEING IT ALL

My search for the truth about my existence has always been part of my life, and the more I progress along this inner journey, the more I realize that I have only delved a small way into the possible realms of experience. As I develop, what I am able to understand changes also.

I remember hearing in one of my psychology lectures about separation anxiety disorder, and with delight called my mum afterwards and explained to her that this was what I had as a child. I had cried with terror every day (yes, every day, ask my parents) for three years when I was made to go to school. Notice I still use the words '*made to go* to school.' As I began to see clearly why I had behaved like this, I took comfort in the knowledge. If you take the inner journey, you will make similar discoveries. The joy is that you learn from them and then move forward in a new way.

Finding a deeper element of yourself to embrace is not only possible, it is a total joy. In my years as a psychologist, I have seen growth in others that has touched me deeply and inspired me. So, embrace every part of where you are and where you are going. It's an experience not to be thrown away.

I'm very lucky to have studied different perspectives of human existence simultaneously. As a student of psychology I learned about the brain, our emotional reactions, how our experiences affect us on an everyday basis and the complex inner patterns which can develop. Alongside this, I learned yogic philosophy, which seemed to offer a very different way of addressing our existence. This taught me the joy of connecting with a deeper part of myself, beyond the chatter of the mind. This can be known as the spirit, the higher self or the universal self. I like to call it the 'real self', because when we allow ourselves to tap into it, that is exactly what we experience: something that is real, beyond the illusions we create with our constant mind chatter. And when we connect to this, we also connect to the greater whole.

Let's learn about the richness of this human experience and divert away from a restricted, egotistical way of being.

PEELING THE ONION

Allowing the real self to shine through is literally like peeling an onion. Our amazing centre is hidden by layers of habit, belief, limiting thought and continual mind chatter. We peel away the layers and there we are…

There are many brilliant and very differing perspectives on how to do this. Let's look at some of the most important concepts.

Let's begin by addressing the experience of the ego. This is the part of us that recognizes distinct differences between us and other people and identifies with the experience of 'I'.

All of our perceptions can bring forth an ego response, as our mind is activated by the stimuli that we receive through our senses and we evaluate those stimuli and act accordingly. Imagine, for example, that you are walking down a familiar road. You stop to look at a new restaurant. You can smell the food, see that the owner is inside and hear the staff talking. You may even get a free taster. You then evaluate this sensory experience — 'The smell of the food is appealing, the restaurant looks clean, the owner is smiling at me' — and your response may be to smile back, book a table, walk away, tell a friend, and so on. The ego will allow you to evaluate this experience in reference to yourself, the 'I': 'I have been in this new restaurant, I like the owner, I have eaten the food, I feel safe and comfortable there, I know about this new restaurant, others do not.'

By acknowledging that a part of us identifies only with the experience of the 'I', we can begin to understand that this part has the potential to make us feel separate from others, and possibly better or worse than others. In fact, we can not only feel separate from others, we can also feel disconnected from whole groups of people we think are different from us. The ego can quite happily reinforce this.

The ego can ignite a defence mechanism. Imagine that you are feeling threatened. How easy is it to feel better about yourself by making a personal judgement, for example:

- *'You are so stupid!'* (You are different and are wrong for not knowing what I do, and I am clever.)
- *'You've never even been there — what do you know?'* (Only I can identify with this and only I know what is right, so you know nothing and I am better than you.)

Don't punish yourself for doing this — this is just a gentle look and learn at the wonder of the human experience.

Sometimes the ego can reinforce an inner desire to be different, so we can separate ourselves from others. The problem comes when we undermine our own happiness by holding on to an identity that says 'I am always having a drama in my life' or 'I am always in pain and you cannot understand this.' We need to understand where these desires stem from.

THE IDENTITY CONFLICT

If I were to ask you to describe yourself to me, what would you say? Who are you? What makes you the person you are?

Personally, I could answer with several different responses: 'I am a wife, daughter, psychologist, writer, yoga teacher, radio presenter. I am a loving person, I am affectionate, I love learning…' The list could go on and on. However, these attributes are not necessarily who I *am*. They are an expression of the *roles* that I take on as part of being Nicola. They are simply what I do in this life.

How much do I rely on these roles to define who I am and whether I'm good enough? If, all of a sudden, I were not, say, a psychologist, how would I feel about myself? How much do I need Nicola to play these roles in order to know who I am?

Now turn your attention to yourself. How much do the roles you play matter to you? To what extent do they make you feel good about yourself? Have you ever lost them, perhaps through redundancy, maternity leave, moving jobs, having children leave home, retiring, choosing to go back to education or even moving to a town where no one knows you? What happened then?

If these roles were to go now, what would be left?

I have often thought about this, because of course the roles I play bring a certain amount of praise, reward and recognition from others. If they were to go, would I feel good about myself anymore?

There have a been a few important situations in my career to date when my ego identified so forcefully with an end result that when it didn't happen I felt crushed. This was because the end result was what I wanted to be identified with. That was all ego-fuelled insecurity. Now I see that achieving that would only have enhanced my own ego mindset and I would have been in danger of thinking that I was better than others. I feel lucky to have seen this so clearly. At the time I did allow myself time to grieve as I shed the illusion of who I thought I was and the role I wanted to play to be 'good enough'. But what I do is not who I am. My inner journey now guides my life and the outer expression of my success comes from a place of peace and joy rather than ego.

Disappointment can hurt, but it sets us free of the rigid pathways we think we should follow and opens up fresh possibilities we never imagined happening for us. Interestingly enough, success is usually the next step along the journey, and it certainly was for me — both the inner success of my learning bringing me closer to the truth of my being rather than just my ego mind, and outer success as a result of this new way of being. And now I am learning to give love and allow it to flow into my life *without* the expectations I had in the past. So I have greater peace in everything I do.

We are far more than the sum of the roles that we play. However, at times we can think that these roles define us, show the world who we are and prove to others what we can do. We are often drawn into the illusion of the role at the expense of embracing the real selves. The irony is that when we let the real self shine out, what does emerge is even more inspiring and incredible.

When we wake up in the morning, we open our eyes to the world, and before that moment kicks in when we remember what we have to do, there we are: our real selves. Notice this moment, cherish it — it is pure awareness of just being in the present moment and at peace.

A great teacher has taught me what happens next: we remember what tasks need to be done and start to put on the metaphorical layers that we have created for ourselves, as if we were putting on clothing. I use the word 'remember', because it is the thinking mind that reminds us 'I am a teacher, I am a wife, I have to make my packed lunch' etc. Notice the 'I'. So we put on our 'I am a teacher' coat, and then more and more layers — all the roles and jobs and expectations that come with being us. That is how we know ourselves.

What roles are you putting on in those moments? And which come with a heavy burden? These could be 'I do everything for everyone and must be needed' or 'I live a very stressed life with no "me" time' or even 'I am a lawyer and must be the best at all costs.'

Whatever your roles, within milli-seconds that connection to who you really are has gone, and the roles you are playing, along with the heavy mindset which comes with them, may not be bringing you happiness. So would it be possible for you to go about your daily life with the intention of staying open to the connection within? Could you *enjoy* the roles that you have created rather than feel you have to live up to them? If you don't feel at your best one day, could you allow yourself to say 'I am good enough and this is the best I can do today' instead of belittling yourself? Can you live from the heart of the onion?

FEELING DIFFERENT

Part of defining who you are is often defining who you are not. Have you ever asked yourself, 'Who do I feel different from?' Just see which people or groups come up. They may include people of different genders, ages, religions, social classes… What about people who are not as good looking as you?! Do you feel different from people who work in charities or run businesses or have different levels of education from you?

Just think about how many millions of people you are separating yourself from. No wonder so many of us feel so lonely — we block out whole groups of people from our lives without really questioning why.

The only thing that separates us from those people is the belief that we are different. Yet this can be very powerful and lead to all sorts of conclusions. If we are right, for example, does that mean that everyone else is wrong? If we are going to heaven, is everyone else going to hell? If we are a victim, is everyone a potential threat?

I'm not suggesting that we all ought to be the same in every area of our lives without expressing our own gifts and ideas — wouldn't that be boring? But wouldn't it be wonderful to embrace others rather than push them away because of their differing beliefs, values, habits and choices?

When we learn how to embrace others for who they are, this can reinforce our connection with ourselves. For if we can see another being simply as part of this incredible world, we can begin to see ourselves as the same.

I personally started this process with small steps of recognition of the connection between myself and others. I would sit on the train and if someone dropped an umbrella and went red with embarrassment, I would say to myself, 'That's something that could happen to me,' rather than 'What an idiot!' If an elderly person or a pregnant woman got on the train, instead of thinking, 'I should give you a seat (but I don't really want to),' I would think, 'If I were you, I would need a seat.' Gradually I learned to smile more at others, judge them less and, most importantly, enjoy more moments of connection. Finally I reached the point where in situations that really tested me, like other drivers cutting me up, I would say out loud, 'You are a beautiful angel!' instead of calling them a rather rude name. It starts with small steps, but gradually we can learn to embrace everyone, no matter what they're doing!

From today, in every situation where you view someone as different from you, see if you can allow yourself a tiny moment of recognition of the connection between you. To begin with, it could be something as simple as 'We are both on the same bus.'

When you separate yourself from others, not only are you not allowing yourself to fully embrace them, you are also not allowing *them* to fully embrace *you*. So stop hiding behind your newspaper and give someone a smile. Allow yourself to open up to the rest of humanity in all its bright and wonderful glory.

UNDERNEATH IT ALL

So much for the ego, now let's turn our attention to the subconscious. This is a powerful part of our mind. It is capable of storing and processing far, far more than the conscious mind. This is why the mind is so frequently referred to as an iceberg: the vast majority of it lies beneath the surface.

One of the regulatory functions of the subconscious is maintaining optimal physical functioning, including controlling breathing rate, blood pressure and movement. You didn't consciously instruct your fingers to turn the page of this book just now, did you?

Your conscious mind can in fact be totally oblivious to the functioning of the subconscious. As the conscious mind focuses on choosing your favourite food, for example, the subconscious may be signalling that this food will make you fat and therefore unlovable. The two minds do not work together, but as parallel systems.

Sometimes the conclusions that come from the subconscious mind may not seem rational to the conscious mind. Once, during a hypnotherapy session where I was addressing why I had allowed myself to experience so much disease, my subconscious was giving the therapist the run-around. Why would I do that when my biggest wish was to be well? But my subconscious thought that by having the disease I would be safe. It was actually looking after me. The subconscious *is* there to look after you. It is working for your highest good. Don't underestimate its power or try to rationalize it. Understanding that is exists is enough.

Sometimes people I am working with question why they remember traumatic events so clearly when they want to forget them. However, they frequently realize that a part of them knew that they had to remember the event so that they could do something about it one day. That's the subconscious at work again. Of course the vivid images do not help these people move away from the pain, but the pact that they made with themselves has worked.

There are many ways of dealing with pain. Other clients filter out their painful memories in order to feel less anger towards their loved ones, or store up their emotional pain, which is then expressed physically as disharmony or disease.

Moving forward from pain is possible. Don't put a restriction on the time involved or pressurize yourself with how far you have to go today; just know that it is possible and today you are doing your best. That is enough.

The subconscious stores our reactions to different sensory stimuli. If you are going on a first date, for example, you may find that a variety of thoughts and reactions come up. It is as if someone is running around that huge subconscious storage system of yours and picking out files for your attention. A few possible data files and their reactions are:

File name: How does my body act when I get nervous?
Reaction: I need to urinate more often.

File name: Last relationship
Reaction: Remembering the pain of the break-up with my ex.

File name: Does my hair look OK?
Reaction: Repetitive hair combing along with thoughts that I am not attractive enough.

Do we really need all this? The subconscious thinks so, but these thoughts are harmful and cannot help us to achieve a peaceful state. But, if the subconscious is so powerful, how can we begin to change the data?

New and consistent suggestions that are fed into the subconscious help to create new data files for us to tap into. These new thoughts help us to divert away from the old data and into new responses to the sensory input that we receive.

If from today you start taking a few deep breaths every time you get anxious, for example, then you are opening a new file called 'What I do in emergencies'. The more you use data from this new file, the more the new action of breathing deeply and slowly to calm yourself down will become familiar. You will reach for it more readily.

Allowing these new ideas to become habitual involves more than just a new state of mind: it requires *emotion*. Emotion allows you to tap into vision, imagination and the feeling that powers up your thoughts with deep recognition. The *idea* of the breaths alone does not resonate with calming down; it is the *experience* of the *emotion* of igniting calm that creates the conditions for change.

I have met many clients who, for varying reasons, have kept a lid on their emotions because they were overwhelming, not safe to have, needed to be contained or were incomprehensible from a rational viewpoint. If this resonates with you and yet you are feeling low, remember *that* is an emotion, and a great foundation to build upon. You are already learning that emotions can be accessed. The next step is to access them in a safe and productive way.

Tapping into emotions is key when making affirmations — positive statements made to create new positive thoughts and beliefs. Have you ever made these and then wondered why nothing is happening? That's because you may be making them with your conscious mind whilst your subconscious focuses on what you are going to make for dinner. In fact, you can be saying 'I am a loving person' whilst focusing on 'I hope I don't miss my bus home.'

Tapping into the emotion of what you are saying will allow the full meaning of the words to be felt. Try it now. Repeat the words: 'I am at peace.' Say them a few times. Say them any way you like — even put an accent on. Now say them again, but this time tap into the *feeling* of peace. Take this feeling deep into your gut and put your heart into creating it within. Do this several times. Listen to how different your voice sounds when there is emotion behind your words.

This also explains why so many people comment that they read self-help books but don't find them helpful or feel a change. How are they reading them? Are they addressing the words or allowing themselves to tap into the meaning of those words *with feeling*? It is through experience we learn and change. You cannot simply intellectualize change; you have to experience it in order to fully embrace change; engage your emotions along with your new thought patterns. This allows you to access your subconscious mind and make powerful shifts in your mindset.

IT'S EVERYWHERE AND EVERYTHING, BUT WHAT IS IT?

As we are discussing the power of our thoughts and emotions, it is time to address what is occurring here: movement of energy.

No matter what discipline we turn to, energy is key. It is everywhere. It has been scientifically proven to exist both in the atmosphere around us and in every one of our cells. We are aware of it all the time, whether we realize it or not. Compare being in the company of someone happy and someone angry, or being in a religious building and in a supermarket.

Take a moment to tap into the atmosphere in the space you are in right now. How does it make you feel? Why does it feel this way? How is it different from other environments?

So, what is energy exactly and how can acknowledging this help us to reclaim happiness?

Quite simply, energy is the universal life force or essence that exists both within us and this whole expansive universe. This force flows within and through us and every other being, animal, object and atmosphere.

One of the greatest physicists of all time, Max Planck, drawing on the genius of Albert Einstein and generations of scientists' work, explains how we must assume that an intelligent consciousness or power exists behind this natural force. This intelligence is key to understanding the workings of our universe. It is the perfection that we experience when we reclaim our real self. We can acknowledge its existence and tap into it and experience it in different ways.

We are all part of something much bigger than our limited selves, whether we choose to acknowledge it or not. Our divine nature is not about believing that something divine is in control of us but embracing ourselves as part of this divine intelligence. For we are all part of this same universe and therefore divine energetic beings by nature.

As we become more in touch with this intelligence within, we can begin to view our experiences to date as being necessary to bring us to where we are today. We can begin to feel connected to other people rather than feel we are a human being who is walking through life as merely a chattering mind and nothing else. More importantly, we can realize that we have the freedom to jump up and take responsibility for creating something new. We are part of a greater whole more than we ever imagined. And we can access a greater connection with all.

So often we are brought up to believe that only certain people can tap into the greater elements of this universe. We may even have been led to believe that questioning what life is all about is wrong. But we are not wrong and neither are the people who told us that. Our path has led us here and their path has led them somewhere else, that's all. We can only focus on our own journey and let them do the same. We don't need others' permission to delve deeper into the elements of our being and embrace a greater connection with all that is.

We can all move beyond the restrictions of our past and embrace the present moment in a new way. If I can, you can. We are the same, remember?! So:

- Are you willing to let yourself experience life with a new spiritual level of understanding?

- Are you willing to let yourself move away from old bought-into beliefs that have not led you to true contentment and happiness?
- Are you willing to open up to the possibility that living your life with a more spiritual level of consciousness could be what you have been crying out for?

Hand in hand, we go forward.

SO, HOW CAN I CHANGE MY LIFE?

You go to a dinner party and someone walks in. Before you have even seen them, you sense their presence. Their charisma is powerful and the room changes. Another person enters. You don't see them either — they are feeling insecure and wish to hide away.

Opening up to the possibility that we can be influencing ourselves, our body and our environment on an energetic level allows us to get an idea of how subtle changes in thought, emotion and behaviour can have a huge impact on every aspect of our experience.

Even when our thoughts aren't spoken aloud, they carry a vibration — the resonance of their energy. Every thought will carry a different vibration. This vibration is powered up by the emotion attached to the thought and sent out into this intelligent universe. Think of radio waves and how listeners are drawn to what is being sent out by the radio station. Similarly, any thought you send out into the ether connects with the same vibrational force within the divine intelligence of the universe. 'Like attracts like' is the simplest way of understanding this concept. You are in fact finding the physical equivalent of your thought energy.

This constant exchange of energetic equivalents shows up in the physical reality around you. It follows, therefore, that positive thought, along with emotion, perseverance and determination, will attract a more positive physical reality into your life.

Developing an attitude of expectancy is key to this process. Expecting an improved physical reality to appear will intensify the thought energy that can make this happen. But it is important that this comes from a feeling of gratitude rather than 'I want, give me now.' That would only reinforce your *wanting* and *needing* rather than your openness to *receiving*. We are not writing a Santa's wish list here but understanding how, as part of this incredible intelligent universe, we can attract and accept what we wish to experience.

Belief is key to the process. If you don't believe that it is going to work for you, then already you have put a stumbling block in your path. And if your emotional input is a feeling of impossibility and failure, guess what you will get?

Let's look at another limiting approach. If someone feels that they are always the victim of others' foul play and continually sends these thoughts out, life will constantly provide situations where they can be just that.

To take a more positive example, the more we are able to adopt a loving, caring approach to every individual we meet, the greater the experience of love we will be open to receiving ourselves. This can almost appear from nowhere when in fact it is merely the 'like attract like' of our thoughts and beliefs.

So we can see that directing our thoughts with emotion, focus and intention creates an extremely fertile ground for the physical match of this energy to manifest. And we are all able to create a physical reality that resonates with the peace, harmony and love that we deserve.

CAN I LOVE MYSELF AS I LOVE YOU?

I see all the clients who come to me as the incredible beings they are. But because they are in pain and suffering and usually don't like themselves, they can't see it. It is like when someone asks, 'Does my bum look big in this?' and you think it looks great, but they can't see it.

Maybe you can't see just how magnificent you are right now, but I am here to tell you that whatever life has brought you, whatever your current beliefs, whatever other people have told you, you are an incredible divine being and you can and do shine. Don't think that you are your past, because you are not — the past is over, remember? Don't think that you are what you have done, because you are not the sum of your actions, you are so much more. Don't think that you are what everyone says you are — you are limitless and lovable and capable of anything. Don't think that you are reading this book to understand how to achieve — you already have it all, you are just not embracing the magnitude of your true incredible nature yet.

What if you could see yourself as being as incredible as the person you love the most? Right now think of that person. Close your eyes and tap into how this love feels. Incredible, huh? How do you think of that person? How do you overlook their irritating habits and quirks of behaviour and still see that they are incredible? That is the extent of love I am talking about. Could you do this for yourself?

Before you even mention the fact that you are not beautiful or incredible, etc., stop for a moment. These are just your old thoughts — does buying into them resonate with inner fulfilment and happiness? Of course not. So you have to make the shift towards thinking in a new way. Change your thought energy and you will see your life change too.

SEEING OURSELVES IN A NEW WAY

Imagine that you wear glasses. The lenses represent how you feel about yourself and the world around you. Today you wake up and put on your 'The world is a terrible place' glasses. You walk down the road and see a piece of litter and this reminds you that people don't care, then someone bumps into you and you have those familiar feelings that everyone makes your life so hard, and then you get to the train station and miss the train by 30 seconds, and here you go again, your day is going from bad to worse and it's only just started.

The next day you wake up and put on your 'I am at peace with myself and my world' glasses. You walk down the same road as yesterday but you don't actually notice the litter today as you are looking at the flowers, or maybe you just put the litter in the bin. Someone bumps into you and says sorry. It's really no problem. You miss the first train, but there's another one coming in only four minutes (a whole 240 seconds) and you're looking forward to the journey because it's time just for you and you can read a book, listen to music, eat and prepare for the day.

What glasses are you wearing right now?

What glasses would you like to wear tomorrow?

Could it be possible that by changing your glasses you not only change your perception of the world but also enable that world to be one of plenty, support and opportunity?

The energy that you are vibrating in your thoughts, speech and actions is the same as the glasses that you are choosing to wear, and, as we have seen, thoughts carry energy and help to create your reality.

As energy is everywhere, the thoughts that you have also create a profound effect on the atmosphere around you — on how people behave towards you, what they sense about you, what situations you are open to and what situations are attracted to you. Why not invite in situations that resonate with happiness?

So far you have probably been giving out that you are not good enough, not skilled enough, need to prove something, are judged by others, are scared even — and what have you created? A reality that resonates with this.

Yesterday a client who missed her appointment due to being up all night with a health condition said to me, 'Oh, I could have killed myself! I hate myself when I do this. I am so angry.' Of course she wasn't being literal about ending her life just because she hadn't seen me. However, it was interesting that she could express such inner hatred towards herself in such a normal manner. You may say that she was angry and we all say similar things when we are angry. But that's the point.

Fortunately, change is a simple process. But in order to change something you must become aware of it. From today, just become aware of what your thoughts are. What are the themes when you are criticizing yourself in your own mind and to others? When are you having thoughts that don't resonate with what you would like to see in your life? Do 'I hate myself' thoughts resonate with accepting love? Do 'I may fail' thoughts resonate with opportunities for success?

I know that at times it isn't easy to look at ourselves, because then we know we have to do something about our situation. The first day I spoke to my husband he said to me, 'You have built a wall around yourself.' He was right and I knew it, but boy, was it hard for me to face up to how my life had turned out because of that wall. So I can assure you from personal experience that the hardest work is over now. The fact that you are reading this book shows that there is a part of you that has faced up to where you are and is open to change.

So, it's time to be a little different…

EXERCISE 1: *Diverting into Something New*

Make sure you have a small amount of undisturbed time. Take a piece of paper and just float around some ideas of what you would really like to experience in your life. What would you love to see occurring? What would bring feelings of happiness, satisfaction, peace and joy?

Write until all your dreams are down in front of you. You may like to list the words, or write random ideas as they come, or draw a picture or diagram — whatever works for you.

Now focus on what you would like to experience *within* yourself. Just think of the behaviour that you would like to divert away from and the more harmonious personality traits, skills and emotions you would like to see flourish.

If you are finding this challenging, then think of those moments when you have seen another person demonstrating a skill, a positive personality trait or form of behaviour and have thought, 'I would like to be like that.' It may have been their inner confidence, their discipline or even their ability to listen to their own gut feelings and act upon them.

Consider also those personality traits, skills and ways of behaving that you feel you would like to top up and experience more frequently. You may feel that you are able to demonstrate patience, for example, but a little more of it would help you to feel calmer and less frustrated. Let your ideas flow until you feel you have covered every aspect of change you can imagine.

Keep this record of your ideas tucked in this book, as we will visit it again.

Chapter 2

Misunderstanding our Personal Power:
Diverting Away from the Influence of Others

Do not go where the path may lead, go instead where there is no path and leave a trail.

—*RALPH WALDO EMERSON*

If you were to compare your list from the exercise that you just completed to someone else's list, no doubt there would be differences. You may never have travelled, for example, and wish to learn from other cultures, while others may have spent their childhood moving from town to town and would like to experience the feeling of stability. I may feel drawn to work with people one way and you another. That's not better or worse, just *different*. We are all expressing our divine selves in a way that feels right for us. And we are all here to learn and grow and love and be happy and fulfilled.

We also all have the opportunity to change. Again, this is a process that is different for us all. So don't compare your rate of change to anyone else's. It is pointless and will only bring additional internal pressure. I see so many clients criticize themselves for not changing quickly enough. This just results in even more frustration and discomfort. So please just let go of any expectations of where you 'ought' to be. The irony is that letting go will open up the space for you to see that you are already there now.

As well as putting pressure on ourselves, so many of us let other people influence us and lead us down paths that do not resonate with our own happiness. Sometimes we can live our whole lives keeping others happy, fulfilled, quiet and proud while sacrificing our own happiness. This is very common, especially within the family. We can even let other people convince us that our way of being and our ideas are wrong. How can this happen?

We can even let others drive our process of change. I have had so many clients who have come to me because a family member or partner has told them to.

For some, this has been through gentle encouragement, but for others it has been through force or pressure, because another person thinks they are wrong or bad. In either case, there is the expectation that they will change to please the other person. The question is, though, if you feel that you are unable to meet another person's expectations, how does that make you feel about yourself? Not very good.

This isn't helped by the fact that we often believe that we know exactly what other people are thinking — especially about us. I have heard clients say other people don't like them or think they are stupid. When I question them on how they know this, I realize they have just drawn wild conclusions based on their own ideas about themselves.

So why is it so common to imagine that others don't see the best in us?

It is because we don't see the best in ourselves.

Think about it — so often we allow another person to tell us we are wrong, or weak, inferior, incapable, and so on, not because we think they know best but because of how we feel about ourselves. The other person is just a pawn in the game of life reinforcing what we already think. They aren't there by chance, but as a reflection of our own energy.

I'm not suggesting that you will never be wrong or misinformed — that is the wonderful learning of life. But when you are living with the constant feeling that you are not good enough, you interpret everyone else's response to you in a way that backs up this idea.

Take a look at the old 'Does my bum look big in this?' question. So often it is posed in order to make up for internal self-criticism. The person really does think their bum looks big and they want someone to tell them that they are wrong. But their subconscious view is so powerful that even if they are told they look great, they will automatically think, 'I know I don't look good, so you must be lying or wrong.' Can anyone ever say the right thing in answer to this question?!

Think of a situation in your life where you asked for another's opinion and then felt hurt by it.

- Why did you ask them in the first place?
- Did you believe what they said?
- Why did it hurt so much?
- If you hadn't asked them, what conclusions would you have drawn for yourself?
- Would this have brought you greater happiness?

Now let's look at a different situation. What are you doing right now? Reading this book, I imagine. Are you criticizing yourself for holding it in a certain way or turning the pages too slowly? Probably not. Why not? The answer is because you were probably never told that there was a wrong way to hold a book or a wrong speed to turn a page. So you accepted that these were things that couldn't be done wrong.

As a child, however, I was picked up on holding a book too close to me by every teacher I had. Everyone thought it was wrong and bad for my eyes. But I needed to hold it close in order not to be confused by the letters I was reading. Even today, as I brought my computer screen very close to my eyes I said to myself, 'Maybe that is a bit too close,' and moved it back a little. I do need it to be close and I do know what I need, I have great eyesight and don't wear glasses, and yet I still just questioned whether I was right.

Now I shall move the screen closer again to be in harmony with my needs!

If we are taught at an early age that something is wrong, we are likely to accept it. This is not to do with being gullible or easily swayed, but because throughout the most important learning years, from conception to about the age of ten (some schools of developmental psychology suggest that it is less, others more), we have no other point of reference, so do not question what we are taught.

Moreover, the people who are teaching us are limited by what they know. They can't teach us to feel calm, happy and connected to everyone with love if they don't know how to be calm, happy and connected themselves. We can't be angry with them for what they don't know. What we can do is break away from that cycle.

If someone once taught you how to feel pain or fear through their inappropriate words and actions, then know that you can learn how to feel safe now. You can feel worthy and move forward in a way that is comfortable for you. This is a point of change for you.

DO THIS FOR YOURSELF

The influence of others can be so strong that we often feel guilty about wanting to believe different things from our parents, even when we are adults ourselves. What do you do right now that is different from how you were brought up? Is there anything you feel guilty about or hide from your parents?

It can be a heavy burden if we feel we are letting our parents down by choosing a different way of life. But whatever we were led to believe, we were all born with our own ideas and inner wisdom. Don't overlook this in order to please others — that would be an injustice to yourself. And remember that no one is wrong here. It is merely the breaking of a cycle that does not resonate with a fully fulfilled self.

The ironic thing is that often parents tell their children what they want them to do, but they don't reinforce this with their own behaviour. This is of course confusing to the child. It's so easy to do it, too. Just the other day someone called my name and I answered, 'What?' I then spoke to my seven-year-old niece, who didn't hear me (or probably wasn't listening), and she said, 'What?' and I said to her, 'No, we say "Pardon?"' There I was, saying one thing and doing another and then telling her she was wrong for doing what I did.

If you are a parent or care-giver, don't be hard on yourself — you are doing something that is incredible. And this can be a great opportunity to listen and watch yourself and see what you are really teaching the children around you. Are you teaching them your own beliefs, along with those that were handed down to you, or are you modelling for them an individual who loves and cares for themselves?

Take a moment to think of a few of the major beliefs you hold about the world, about money and relationships, about marriage, about other cultures, about other social classes or groups or religions.

- Where did you learn these beliefs?
- Which of your parents or major life influences thinks the same as you do now?
- Have you ever discussed this belief with this individual in order to understand why they developed it in the first place?
- Have you ever thought that this belief might not resonate with how you *really* feel about the world?

Sometimes we take on others' beliefs quite unconsciously. We may find ourselves living in fear of poverty, for example, when we have never experienced it ourselves. However, our parents may have done so. If this is the case, it's important for us to know that we can break the cycle and claim our birthright of feeling safe and secure and deserving of abundance. Making this active choice to move away from thoughts and beliefs that hold us in old family, socio-economic and habitual cycles will help us to feel free and light. Ultimately, we will be able to drop the baggage of others' experiences and reclaim our own inner happiness.

At other times, rather than taking on others' beliefs, we are so fearful that we are going to become like our parents, teachers and care-givers that we behave very differently from them in order to prove to ourselves that we are not like them. Children raised with very angry parents, for example, often hold their anger within.

However, we don't need to hide anything that is part of us for any reason. We can learn that it is safe to express emotions. We are much greater than our learned behaviour and thoughts.

'IT WAS JUST SO LONG AGO...'

Family cycles are often so ingrained that we hardly recognize that we are following the same path as our immediate family, or even our distant ancestors. It's amazing to think that we can hold beliefs right now that go back to people we have never even met, but due to the cycle of learning and passing on we can find ourselves doing just that.

Take a moment to cast your mind back over the discussions that were familiar in your childhood. Was the world seen as a hard place that never gave people like you a break? Was there a general belief that you had to work hard, even struggle, to get through life? Think about the experiences that may have shown up in your own life to reinforce this struggle. Would your family ideas make you want to embrace life, fear it, feel persecuted by it or want to hide from it?

Suffering, anger and prejudice can be passed down the generations, but we don't need to continue the pattern. So often, people hold the belief that by carrying family pain they are in some way punishing someone for a past wrong or making sure that no one forgets. But the only person they are punishing is themselves. If someone from a previous generation experienced pain and suffering then we can help them by sending them love, whether they are alive or have passed on, and having compassion for them. In this way, we — and future generations — can step away from old hurts that are not even ours to carry. We can let the present moment be about *our* journey of life rather than pain long gone.

We don't need to feel guilty about wanting to be free of the ties of our family's past, or as though we are a traitor for seeing the world as a good place. We don't need to feel we aren't a good son, daughter, sibling or cousin for not wanting to continue a family cycle of pain. We are in fact allowing a fresh perspective to flow into a stale situation.

We can give ourselves permission to think about our own life experience, our ancestors and the whole world in a new way. We just have to allow ourselves to find comfort in peace rather than familiarity in separation.

'DON'T DO IT!'

As we try and move to something new, however, we may find that limiting thoughts and beliefs become exaggerated, both in our own mind and in our relationships with others. This can make us frustrated or even angry. We want to change, but another part of us seems determined not to let it happen.

We can actually scare ourselves out of change by imagining the reaction of other people. It amazes me how it is possible to have huge battles with people in our own head. They even answer back! Clients often describe to me lengthy rows they have imagined that will never happen in reality.

Sometimes rows do happen in reality, though. Others may try and discourage us from changing because the way we are right now is serving them by keeping *them* from changing. Imagine, for example, that you and your friends always have a weekly night out in a local bar. One night you suggest that instead you all go bowling. Some of your friends may welcome the change, but others may not. You are asking them to step out of their comfortable routine and embrace something new.

So, if you are embarking on this path of personal change expecting everyone around you to fully encourage you, be aware that this may not happen. I say 'may', because you may be fully supported by everyone in your life. However, you may not. Some may even discourage you. They are not bad, they are not wrong, they are just where they are, and we cannot criticize them for needing to feel safe or secure in their old patterns, just send them the love that we ourselves would like to feel.

There may also be parts within ourselves that want to continue the way we are in order to feel secure. For the moment, though, let's just stay with the reactions of other people. When we choose to embark on something new, those who wish to stay in their place of fear and pain will try and hold us in that place also. Have you ever heard the saying 'Misery likes company'? Well, that can be said for suffering as a whole. I'm not suggesting that others will hold us in a place of suffering to deliberately cause us pain; it is just part of the processing and patterns that they are not aware of. To take a literal example, if someone is scared of going camping in the forest, they may tell us about the potential dangers and threats in order to make us afraid to go as well.

There are many different patterns that can be used to discourage change. Guilt is an old one, but a favourite for many. ('What will I do when you're gone?' 'I didn't bring you up to behave like this!') A little bit of reinforcing your old behaviour can occur. ('Just one cigarette won't hurt you.' 'What's got into you these days? I'll be happy when you're back to your old self.') There might even be a good helping of totally unsupportive behaviour. ('You can start eating healthily if you like, but I'm not going to be buying all that expensive food.' 'It's your life — don't come running to me when it all goes wrong.') I'm sure some of these sound familiar.

So we may feel that change is hard because we will have to face up to other people's reactions along the way. Throughout this book I'm going to show how you can stay centred within yourself at such times. This will make the process much easier. For now, just recognize that these are individuals who themselves are not fully at peace and are therefore not at ease with you changing in order to find peace. It is as if you're sending out a ripple of energy that something new is on the way and not everyone is ready to accept it. It's that simple really.

LETTING OTHERS IN — TO NOURISH US

If we find ourselves surrounded by people who don't resonate with our desire for peace and fulfilment, it's worth asking whether these people are serving our highest good. Are *we* serving our highest good by being in the company of those who are not going to assist us on this journey?

I'm not suggesting that we dispense with the advice of those who are helpful and supportive. But how do we decide who is offering us the best advice?

Imagine I said that in order to change you had to tie a blue balloon to your ear every day. You would probably think I were a little insane. If I were to say that learning to move away from anger would help you to find peace, you might take me more seriously. That would sound possible or even right, wouldn't it? Well, you've just made the distinction between what feels right for you and what doesn't. Learning to tap into these feelings will help you to evaluate the advice you are given.

I could write a whole book on listening to your intuition, and further chapters will offer more ways to do this. It really is as simple as saying, 'What feels right for me?'

To put this thinking into place right now, let's look at the ten main reasons why we let others influence us. With each one, think of a situation where you may have done this. Then take a moment to think about how it made you feel. Did you move towards happiness and fulfilment or feel that you had compromised your heart's desire?

1.   Other people know what is right for me, so I let them make decisions for me or constantly seek their approval.
2.   My past decisions haven't led to positive outcomes, so I let others make decisions so that I don't have to.
3.   I am indecisive, so I let others make decisions for me.

4. I don't know what to do with my life, so I let others make decisions for me.
5. My decisions lead to pain, so I don't want to make them anymore.
6. I need someone else to back me up in what I am doing.
7. I am not sure who I really am, so I let others guide me so that my path is already mapped out.
8. I am doing this to please someone else, even though it doesn't bring me fulfilment, rest or peace.
9. I don't think that I am as good as other people, so I don't follow my inner path in case I do it wrong or fail.
10. It is easier to go along with what others want rather than questioning what is right for me. I want an easy life.

Now before you read on, review these ten statements again. This time think about how you would feel if you trusted that you and your path were already perfect. Just try a few statements and see the difference.

If you had this trust, you wouldn't seek out approval or try to please others, or use them as an excuse not to change. You would allow yourself to move away from old patterns because you were worth it. Well, aren't you worth it now?

'DO AS I SAY!'

Let's flip this on its head. We can also try to control others with *our* ideas about how *they* should be. We want them to fit in with our beliefs, values and expectations. Maybe you are a parent and you want your child to have the very best life, so you insist they go to university, even though they want to travel the world. Maybe you want your partner to get a promotion so that you will have more money and feel safer. Maybe you want your friends to take up hobbies so that you don't have to do them alone, even though they aren't really interested. Maybe you think that your way of doing things is the only way, so you won't let your family or friends try something different without a fight. Maybe your beliefs are so strong that the fact that someone could believe something different seems ridiculous.

Take the time to observe yourself and notice (with kindness, not criticism) when you are doing this. When you catch yourself dismissing someone's ideas, why not question them and try and understand them instead? The experiences that have led them to think as they do may parallel yours in many ways, even though the end result is different.

If you find yourself trying to inflict your beliefs on your loved ones, why not take a moment to remember that their way of doing things may be different from yours and that is OK. Don't be angry if your children want to be different — after all, if they are questioning the world they inhabit and making their own decisions, you have done your job perfectly. It would be a shame to teach children about the wonder of the world, only to restrict what parts of it they can and can't embrace. That includes embracing other people too. How often have race, religion, social status, sexual preferences and many other perceived differences got in the way of possible friendships and ultimately love? Too many!

Ultimately, of course, you cannot change other people, as change has to come from within them, when they are ready, at their pace and in their own time. 'Nicola, I know that,' everyone says. 'You can't change others, you can only change yourself.' True, we know it, but the reality is that we get frustrated watching people we love stay in pain as we move toward a place of well-being. We can even lose touch with our own process of change and just focus on what others aren't 'doing right'.

If you are frustrated by someone else's pain, then remember that by changing your own life you can show them that change is possible. Your inner glow may be enough to show them that there is another way. You don't need to preach to them, or even teach them. If they ask you for help then share with them. But the rest really is up to them.

'WHAT WILL THE NEIGHBOURS THINK?'

Feeling accepted seems to feature so highly in our lives. We set such great store by how others perceive us. We often want to control what they think and to portray ourselves as perfect and in control. Maybe right now you are doing this, even amongst people you would count as close acquaintances. Do you let them see the real you?

I have worked with truly talented and successful people, and so many times they have told me that one day people will find out that they really are a fraud because they aren't good enough. They believe they are fooling everyone into thinking they are good at what they do. They try and control other people's view of them by going that extra mile, even helping others to their own detriment. So often they never let down their guard and show their true emotions, even when the situation allows them to be relaxed, vulnerable, heard and supported. What are they trying to prove? That they are perfect. And why? Because they don't believe they *are* perfect.

So often people, feel that if they show their real self or true feelings they will be criticized by others. If we aren't feeling good about ourselves and are therefore judging ourselves very harshly, then of course we are going to presume everyone is doing the same. But they are not. And no matter what we do or say, we are unable to control what people think and feel about us anyway.

If you feel that you are trying to live up to some unrealistic expectations that you have created for yourself, just take a break and give yourself permission to show people, little by little, the real you. And then you can relax and feel happier. It takes much more effort to hold yourself in a restricted role than just to be yourself.

Similarly, many families have portrayed themselves as stereotypically perfect while the reality behind closed doors has been very different. If this is your own family, remember you don't have anything to hide. Who you are right now is good enough and full of the potential for greatness.

So often we are brought up to do the 'right' or even 'expected' thing that we grow up with the idea that acting in a certain way will result in others viewing us as a good person. Society as a whole can also be an influencing factor. We can feel that following trends or buying into a set of values set by someone else can bring us happiness. But this can ultimately only lead to pain and disappointment. Don't let yourself be swept away by an unachievable illusion that can tie you into a lifetime's struggle. Wouldn't it be better to feel great with who you are and what you have in the now?

None of us need keep up a perfect image any longer. It doesn't serve us in reclaiming true happiness. It also binds us to the illusions and often rigid patterns in life that we have created in order to feel OK. So the anxiety about being found out can go. We have nothing to hide. We can relax and focus on creating an authentic new life for ourselves knowing that we are good enough.

EXERCISE 2: *Creating from our Real Self*

Take your record of where you would like to see your life going and how you would like to be.

For each and every point of change that you recorded, you are going to address whether this desire for change comes from your own self. It may be that your list also contains beliefs, values, expectations, fears, worries, social pressures or even traditions that others have placed upon you.

As you work through your list, write either 'within' for those ideas that you feel are coming from within you, or 'another' for those you feel are not fully your own choice.

Here are some questions to help you before you begin:

- Has this always been a burning desire of yours or are others telling you it's something you should do or have?
- Have you often felt that this aspect of your life or self was just 'enough', not 'good'?

- Does your career choice come with any family pressures or obligatory traditions?

Another way to address this would be to ask yourself: 'Who would I be making happy if I was/did this? Myself or another person?'

This is not a blaming exercise, just a way of distinguishing where your true desires lie. If you find that some of your choices are about making other people happy, making yourself feel needed, keeping others quiet or seeking their approval, then just make a note of this.

EXERCISE 3: *Turning Beliefs into Reality*

Remember that thoughts and emotions are a powerful combination. So, for each point on your list that is your personal choice, create a short positive statement in the present tense that resonates with what you actually want to experience. This has to resonate with you personally, so don't feel there is any format at all, but to guide you, here are some examples:

Concept of Change	New Statement
To be decisive	'I enjoy being a decisive person.' 'My decisions come from a clear point of knowing what is right for me.'
To write	'I now embrace myself as a professional writer and am taking steps towards making this happen.'
To be self-confident	'Each day I feel more confident and worthy.'
To have friends	'I love learning to embrace new friendships.' 'My life is filled with loving, caring and supportive people.'

Continue to do this until you have covered every point on your list and make sure that you have also included liking, nourishing, caring for and even (dare I say it) loving yourself. However foreign this may feel, it is time that you gave yourself permission to see the best in yourself. So, what do you do with these statements? First of all, write them out again on another sheet of paper.

Now look at them and gauge whether you feel any resistance towards any of them. If there is resistance, then either change the statements to ones that feel better (without losing the positive intention and present tense) or add another statement to the bottom which resonates with: 'Starting today, as I move through this change process all resistance leaves me.'

Now read them out loud.

Now read them again and this time add in some emotion. Tap into the feeling of the words. How it would *feel* to embrace self-worth or inner strength, for example?

Keep doing this and listen to how your voice changes as you tap into the feelings. It may help to imagine you are able to draw up some positive feelings from your abdomen area which you can use each time you repeat these statements.

To begin with, just have a few days' reading these affirmations to yourself out loud, or in your head if you are in a public place. Ten times a day is good start. 'Ten times, Nicola, are you joking?' I hear you say. But think about how often your old habitual thoughts go round your head — possibly thousands of times!

Still don't think you have the time? How about if every time you go to the bathroom you read your affirmations?

There are many ways of incorporating them into your life. You can sing them to yourself in the shower. You can pick one and say it to yourself as you walk down the road. You can write them out again and put a copy of them on your mirror or next to your bed and in your pocket or in your wallet so that not only can you read them easily, but each time you reach into your pocket they are there as a reminder of the new thought vibrations that you enjoy using. You can write them out every day if you prefer, tapping into the meaning of the words as you copy them. You can pass them through your mind at the times and places when you find yourself most susceptible to feeling the opposite. When you are getting ready to go out, instead of the usual criticisms you could say to yourself, 'I am learning to love the way I look.' Find the way that works for you and begin to *feel* the change each time you say your affirmations.

Anytime you feel low, remind yourself that you can now draw upon a different thought that can elicit a different feeling — a good feeling, a feeling that brings a new vibration within you and ultimately sends that new vibration back out to the whole universe.

Chapter 3

Misunderstanding our Safety, Stability and Illusions:
Diverting Away from Fear

I count him braver who overcomes his desires than him who conquers his enemies; for the hardest victory is over self.

—*ARISTOTLE*

Fear is a response that all of us have felt at some time to differing degrees. Though it can alert us to danger, it may be holding us back in life. Looking within and discovering the root of a fear can be an empowering experience. Here are five steps which can help us to do this:

1. Acknowledgement
Acknowledging a feeling that is not resonating with peace and calm within and identifying it as fear, or even panic, will help you to understand what is happening within you. Acknowledge, too, that this state may not necessarily be beneficial on your pathway to peace. As you become your own observer, you can begin to see the power in watching your own tendencies to demonstrate fearful thoughts and behaviour.

2. Understanding
Allow yourself the compassion and kindness you would give to a loved one who was afraid. Rarely do we show ourselves the care we give others when we are in desperate need. Remind yourself that everything will be OK and create a space for calm to move in.

3. Reflection
Look at how this fear has affected your life — your beliefs, behaviour, relationships, career, achievements and the way that you feel about yourself.

4. New patterns

Learn how to draw on new thought patterns to ignite feelings of safety and security. Learn instant anxiety-releasing techniques and develop new long-term perspectives to move towards feeling at ease in yourself and your life.

5. Progress

Use your new awareness to move away from limiting negative reinforcements of fear and towards embracing the world safely. You don't need to think of this as a rigid five-point plan, rather the five major points of learning that we will encounter as we continue through this chapter.

'I'M TRYING TO COPE...'

When we are afraid or under extreme pressure, what do we do? One way or another, we try to cope. Unfortunately, our coping mechanisms may not actually deal with the pain or anxiety or panic, and may limit us in other ways.

This process starts in childhood. In our early years, when we haven't yet made sense of the world around us, we don't have a huge store of helpful information and behaviour we can draw on to ease the pain, and just have to do the best we can. This may include shutting down emotions, making up for one weakness by gaining expertise in another area, remembering every bit of pain vividly to deal with later, converting emotional trauma into physical symptoms, self-harming and self-hatred.

It doesn't have to be a huge traumatic event that leads us to formulate these coping mechanisms. Never downplay what you have experienced, for if it has been enough to make you feel sad, low or fearful, then it has affected you. So pat yourself on the back, knowing that you are strong and have done your best. Now is the time, however, to move away from the pain of the past.

It is very common for us to cope by trying to control our life. If we feel that we are in control then we don't have to open up to further pain. And if something traumatic happens, we will be prepared. This can, however, lead to a whole array of addictive avoidance behaviours. I myself spent years over-exercising, starving myself, isolating myself, taking drugs and constantly trying to hide myself away from my real anxieties and fears. None of these experiences came remotely close to bringing me true peace — they were all avoiding the real issue. However, they all helped me experience different parts of myself and I am very grateful for them. I have no regrets — the past is over and I needed those experiences to know what I do now.

You, too, can learn from the past and use it to move forward in a positive way. There are many inspirational examples out there. For instance, One in Four is an incredible charity run by survivors of sexual abuse to help other victims. Never underestimate your strength. You are far stronger than you think.

So let's make a start. Take the time to answer these questions:

- What aspects of your life help you to feel safe, in control and protected?
- What must or mustn't you do to keep that feeling of control or safety?
- What happens when you can't do this? How do you feel then?
- When others question why you have to have things a certain way, how do you react? Do you get angry, defensive, upset, judgemental?

If you have created often time-consuming, rigid patterns of coping, just know that it is safe now to look at the real issues behind them. Be kind to yourself. Give yourself time and patience, and definitely no criticism for this pain you are feeling.

Also, if you are reading this book whilst living in a threatening or even potentially threatening situation, please remember that you are cared for and there is help for you in your area. A small step can make a huge change in your life.

Let's go back to the beginning now and revisit the notion of how we learn. Imagine a child is stung by a bee. Through this direct experience, they begin to develop their own internal store of associations around bees. The incident could be a powerful enough trauma to elicit a fear of flowers, pain, wasps, insects and buzzing noises, to mention just a few, especially if adults reinforce this at the time. It is important to remember that we can develop a store of reactions to an incident that can be extremely different from the original event, and often seem irrational. Why would a bee sting elicit a fear of flies or other insects that don't even hurt us? That is the power of association.

One of the joys of studying psychology is that you get to read about ridiculously unethical experiments that have been conducted in the name of research, usually feeling complete amazement they were ever undertaken. One that is engrained in my mind involved a very loud noise being made behind an infant boy in order to scare him. (He was the son of a nurse, who had given her permission for the experiment.) It went to plan and each time the noise was made, the child became more and more scared. Then, each time the noise was made, the researchers would present a variety of objects — household items, soft toys — to the child. This continued until the child was able to produce a fear response to the random objects without the loud noise, thereby showing the power of association. Of course, the child was then systematically desensitized back to making healthy associations with the objects and the noise. (I really do hope!)

This controlled experiment portrays so perfectly how we can become hyper-sensitive to various stimuli when we are sacred. Think now of something that makes you feel even mildly fearful. Then think of the variety of situations in which this can affect you. Are you afraid of social situations of all kinds, for instance, or just the ones associated with speaking in front of others? Are you just uncomfortable in small closed rooms or does this extend to aeroplanes, cinemas and elevators?

What is actually happening in moments of fear? Unless we are actually in a threatening situation, it is the memories and the perceived threat of discomfort or terror that we are responding to. Our response can be just as strong as when we are faced with a 'real' threat, however. When telling me of traumatic experiences, many of my clients shake, cry and are terrified, even when the original incident took place 50 years before.

You may feel, of course, that your fears don't affect you in your daily life to any great extent and so this isn't a real issue to address. However, this is like building a house on the side of an active volcano thinking it will never actually erupt. Your birthright is to feel happiness and joy, so please allow yourself to move closer to this point. And if you take a glance at your whole life then you may realize that your fears are restricting you more than you think. Underlying fears can have a very powerful effect on us.

Very often when faced with an actual feared situation, or even a terrifying re-minder, we allow ourselves to remain in the pain rather than move our focus else-where. I don't believe that this is because we want to seek out pain or punish ourselves (although that does occur frequently), but because we have forgotten that peace is possible or we simply don't know any other way to react. We may feel powerless and believe we're not strong enough, good enough or even deserving enough to move away from suffering.

Whatever you may have learned from your family and subsequent experiences, please listen carefully: we can all learn how to move away from fear and discover a new way of being.

Diverting away from fear doesn't just make us feel better, but also enables us to see the world is a new way. We may realize that some of our fears are in fact illusions. We can feel that our life is uncertain, for instance, or even in a state of complete up-heaval or crisis, when it is not. We can feel that others are out to judge us when they are not. Seeing the reality of a situation can release us into a place of safety.

Diverting away from fear can also lift the barriers that prevent us from reclaiming happiness. If in your heart you want to work for a charity, for example, but you are afraid of giving up your current salary, then once you have addressed the fear you can begin to move forward.

'THEY TOLD ME SO...'

A few years ago, on the way to teach a workshop entitled 'Living Fearlessly', I came across a magazine called *The Daily Terror*. I took it to my workshop to highlight how easily we can digest fear. I said to the participants, 'How would you feel if you had read this at the beginning of your day?' If they really had read it, and believed everything in it to be true, they would have viewed the world as a scary and volatile place. They might not have left the house!

We can terrify ourselves each day by surrounding ourselves with news of horrific ordeals, crimes and statistics about how likely we are to die of random violence. When I was studying criminal psychology, our lectures were in the evening. Whilst studying rape we were given some statistics on its frequency, including the most common day of the week it occurred. Low and behold, that was the night of our lectures. I remember walking home that evening feeling absolutely terrified. There I was, a rational(ish) woman who, from one piece of information, had allowed her thoughts to cascade into a whole barrel-full of fears and had become hyper-aware of noises and shadows. I have no idea whether the statistics were relevant to the UK, or even true data, but a part of me believed them to be true and my reactions followed on accordingly. Never underestimate the power of what you believe!

How much of what you read, watch, talk about and focus on could lead you to feel immense terror? I am not suggesting that we ignore the problems of the world here, but if we all react with fear, we will never find solutions. Instead we can choose to turn our attention towards serving others rather than continually getting caught up in the drama of life. If I hear of a tragedy, for example, my thought is simply, 'How can I serve to make it better?' The divine expression of humanity is love, so serving others with love seems the simplest and most effective way to help. Every time a police car, ambulance or fire engine rushes by, for instance, I give those people my love and send a silent message of support in the emergencies that they encounter.

So often, however, our reaction to the world is fear because we have been taught this by our parents and primary influences. These people may have thought that they were keeping us safe by instilling these ideas. Or they may even have been try-ing to tell us how wonderful the world was, but their own behaviour was far more powerful in teaching us fear.

These early influences can have lasting effects. If we have repeatedly been told we are 'no good' or 'a waste of space' or even that someone wishes we had never been born, we may never allow ourselves to get close to anyone in case they discover we really are no good. Or we may sabotage everything that *is* good in order to reinforce that we are *not* good, become obsessed with proving that we *are* good, or even seek everyone else's approval, as we don't believe we are good enough to know what to do with our life.

If our parents also believed that *they* weren't good enough, or were even fearful of the world they had created, we might end up thinking some of our fears are normal, as everyone else seems to have them. But remember that we can step outside our family patterns and leave behind any learned behaviour that is holding us back.

As you answer these next questions, I want you to remember that you are just looking in from an observer's perspective and right now you are safe and secure.

- What was it that you learned to fear?
- What did others teach you to fear?
- What do you think about that fearful situation/object/person? (Listen to your everyday speech. Imagine you are describing this fear to your most trusted friend. What words do you use?)
- What do you believe to be true about the fearful situation/object/ person?

Now just imagine for a moment that you could view this object or situation in a different way. Some of the beliefs that you are holding may feel true and strong, but remember that they are not serving you in your pursuit of happiness or peace.

'THEY'RE OUT TO GET ME'

The *Jaws* movies, these great cinematic creations, had the wonderful strap line 'Don't go into the water', which is a great way to reinforce the idea that something is lurking around just to attack you. Humans don't actually taste that good to sharks, but yet again we are talking about a perceived threat.

It is very common for us to perceive that other people, animals and even situations are out to get us. But this just leads to living in a constant state of fight or flight hyper-vigilance. We may be engaging in a constant struggle to prevent the undesired situation from ever occurring. We may be afraid it will happen at any moment and walk around on red alert. We may develop a whole variety of associated fears. (Remember that rather unethical experiment with the young boy?) Or, like many people, we may fear that someone will discover something about us that we are desperately trying to hide.

Take a moment now to look at your life. Think of the activities and places that you are not letting yourself experience. Think of the dreams that you would like to live out but are holding back from. Think of the relationships you aren't fully engaging in. Imagine yourself as an observer and just take a few moments to picture what your life would be like if you did feel that you were safe, secure, stable and worthy in every way.

What would you be doing that you aren't doing now?

THE END – OR IS IT?

I really could have filled up this whole chapter quite easily with stories of fears I have had. I could fill entire volumes with them! One that I will share is how I have felt about death. I don't fear my own death — I actually feel that it is something to be embraced as a new way of experiencing myself. People often find this hard to believe, but it is true. I don't see my death as an end or an escape, merely a complete merging with the divine. However, I have had deep fears concerning other people passing.

My fear began when two people, totally unrelated to each other, whom I dearly loved, were killed, both in car accidents. These happened relatively close together and shook me to the core. I learned that people I loved could disappear and that was final and I was just left behind in pain. This led to being afraid of people I loved dying. And then to being afraid to love. What if I were to get close to someone and then they died?

I am so grateful that the incredible work of Elisabeth Kübler-Ross quite literally fell into my lap. I recommend her books to all who are wishing to understand the death and grieving process. Also, as my study of yogic philosophy continued, I received the great gift of understanding the journey of the divine self to a greater extent. I learned that beyond my life in this body, I already *was* all that there was to be, and my physical body was the vehicle for this wonderful authentic self.

You may be thinking, 'She reached out in blind faith because she was in pain.' I agree that in order to be open to a new concept we do need to be at least willing to put our faith into a new way of being. However, my willingness to embrace new ideas led me to go back to my meditation, my practice of going within, and therefore to experience something new for myself. As we have already noted, this is key to reclaiming happiness: experiencing change, not merely intellectualizing it. Through my own experiences I now see the perfection of the full journey of life and death. It is a gift.

The many spiritual paths of this world offer such differing ideas about God, death and the afterlife or next life. It is good for us to see that a variety of belief is possible and to recognize that we are for some reason choosing one over another.

- What have you been taught about God, death and the afterlife, and by whom?
- Do these ideas bring you peace?
- Do these beliefs reinforce your suffering in life and death?

I'm not here to force you into changing your ideas or religion — that doesn't interest me at all. No discipline is better than any other at bringing peace, love and happiness, and you are free to find the one that works for you. I am only aiming to show you that the ideas you have about death will be having an impact on your life.

If you are holding the belief that you will be judged after death, for example, are you going to be judging every action that you and everyone else takes in life? If you feel that death is final, are you going to be living your life as if time is a desperate issue? If you feel that this life is about suffering but when it ends things will be better, are you embracing suffering without seeing that joy could be an option?

Fearing death can impact your whole life. But if you are willing to experience a feeling other than discomfort when you think about death, then you can begin to move beyond the fear.

There is a big difference between finding safety in staying with familiar beliefs and finding it in choosing to be part of who you actually are in all your glory right now. Which will you allow yourself to accept?

FEARING OTHER PEOPLE

The more I separate myself from you, the more I feel you are different from me. And difference can breed fear. So let's once again think about how we can embrace our neighbour, not fear them.

If we identify very strongly with separation from others, we may feel the need to prove our differences. As we have seen, this can be led by fear that we aren't good enough and we can find ourselves maintaining an image in order to prove ourselves to others. We then fear people finding out that, underneath it all, we aren't as happy as we pretend to be or that we are really just the same as everyone else.

And what would happen if we were to lose any of these things that we need to prove who we are? What if we were to lose our money, our job, our new car? How would we feel about ourselves then? Surely this is not the way to happiness.

SHUTDOWN

Also, the more we lock into rigid belief systems that prescribe one way (only) to be right, successful or a good person, the easier it is to fail or get it wrong. And, in the meantime, it is so time-consuming and tiring to live according to these rules that creativity, free expression and sometimes joy become impossible.

- What do you have to do in order to feel that you are a good person?
- How tight are these restrictions?
- Do you feel that you need to have a drama in your life to feel relevant?
- Do you have to act only in a supportive way when really you want to tell people what you think? Do you fear being rejected for your opinions?
- Do you feel that letting others see your emotions will make them think you are weak?
- Do you think that moving away from your family's way of doing things will mean that they won't love you?
- Do you think that moving away from your current beliefs about God or the universe will mean that you will be punished?

The clients I see are often exhausted by their constant inner battles between what is right and wrong, and what is expected, appropriate or even allowed. Going into total emotional shutdown is common. The ultimate shutdown is depression.

The problem is that many people become so frustrated with themselves when they are low or depressed that they reinforce this by further self-criticism. This then becomes a vicious cycle. If you find that your own pattern is to shut down, don't use anger to get yourself to change. Start by loving yourself.

A client once came in with an elastic band around her wrist. I asked her why it was there and she explained that she had been told that every time she had a negative thought she should ping it as a reminder not to do it — even when she was experiencing fear and rejection. Can you imagine that was really helping her in any way?

We cannot change by being hard on ourselves. We *can* change by learning to love ourselves as we journey towards seeing ourselves as incredible.

A TIME TO LEARN

I see life as an opportunity to learn and grow. Learning comes in many ways, and if we all had expectations of only learning in comfortable situations, we would never learn anything at all.

In my early twenties I had to have many gynaecological procedures. One day I arrived at a nice hospital, got prepped into one of those lovely medical gowns and was led into a room by a rather flustered red-faced nurse who was pretending to be calm. I was nervous and scared but, as you know, we can become very used to painful and feared experiences after a while. I sat next to the bed, as it hadn't been made up yet, and just watched what was happening in the room.

Two nurses were running around in a state of panic, fearful that things would run late and go wrong and the consultant would come down and be angry with them. The schedule was so busy that they couldn't fit everyone in, nothing was going right and they were sure they would be to blame, as no one cared about them anyway.

For some reason a profound calm came over me — even today I can't explain why — and I could see the effect that these two nurses were having on themselves. It was as if they were wrapped up in dark cloud swirling around them and their fear was intensifying it. I could see them feeding off each other's panic and the room becoming ever more stuffy and uncomfortable. I could see the fear was blinding the nurses to the reality of their situation and even to my presence in the room. In a moment of huge realization I could see that I, too, could easily become engulfed in the dark cloud of panic just by tuning into it. I could become that same unconscious insanity.

Without any conscious decision I closed my eyes and all of a sudden I felt different. I felt I had found a calm and centred part of myself and fear did not have to exist, even though the situation almost called for it. When the doctors came, I even remember how ridiculous they sounded as they tried to figure out why I was in pain. I could see and hear clearly because I was calm, and allowing myself to stay calm had an impact on the nurses too.

This was a pretty profound day for me because I began to see how my own fear could be paralyzing to myself, others and my whole life. Up until then, fear had been a major part of my life. I am still learning how to move away from it and embrace greater peace. Let's look at how you can do that too.

THE GIANT SNOWBALL

If you are in a situation that is making you afraid, first, do address whether you need to find safety in a new location until the threat has gone. If the fear is more a theme of your mind chatter, then the simplest thing is to leave the mind chatter too!

Think about the power a thought can generate when we give it our full focus. Imagine a small coin-sized snowball gaining momentum as it rolls down a mountain, getting bigger and bigger until it is the size of a house. It's the same with our snowballing thoughts. You can be having a general chat with a friend and they mention that they have been given a pay rise and you think:

> 'I'm happy for them, but why can't I be as lucky as they are? I never have a job with such good money. I'm never going to be able to pay my debts and get my own house and in the meantime it's impossible for me to bring anyone back to this place, and so who on Earth is going to want me, me with no prospects and no hope? I might as well just stay indoors until 2020, when I'll be too old to do anything anyway.'

Do you see how in under ten seconds we can go from 'I am unlucky' to 'I will always be alone'? It's the 0 to 60 of limiting beliefs. These then feed the negative emotions in this vicious cycle.

The importance of knowing about this is that we can begin to become aware of when we are doing it and the negative snowballing themes that are common to us. And then we can put a big brick in the way of that snowball hurtling down the mountain.

Whenever you feel your thoughts start snowballing, just stand back as an observer and see what happens. Then think of a word or a short phrase that resonates in some way with cancelling this stream of thought. You are not going to be horrible to yourself or say you are wrong, just *divert your mind elsewhere*. Using your own name or a short phrase can be a powerful way to do this. Here are some examples that my clients and I have created:

- 'Nicola, enough now.'
- 'Peace now.'
- 'Back to calm.'
- 'Enough.'
- 'I cancel this thought.'
- 'Stop.'
- 'Nicola, you are safe.'
- 'No more energy on that.'
- 'Let it go.'
- 'Cancel.'

To make this even more memorable, you can use a different voice from your own. Use one that pleases you and ignites a feeling of safety, nurturing or peace.

Remember the power of emotion and thought together? You could in theory spend a whole day saying, 'Cancel,' and nothing else, but that is merely the brick in the way of the snowball. The change occurs as you bring yourself back to a state that resonates with what you want to *feel*: calm and at peace.

Try this technique and stick with it. Change the phrase when you feel it doesn't resonate with you and learn the times when you need it most.

IT'S A WONDERFUL PRESENT

Whenever memories have the potential to upset us, we can move our mind back to the present moment to create a different sensation. This is also what we are doing with cancelling our snowballing thoughts, of course — we are moving into the now.

Whenever we feel that fear or discomfort is overcoming us, another way to draw ourselves back to the present moment is by taking four deep breaths. Yes, it's that simple. Try it now. Just breathe in through your nose, watch the breath fill up your lungs and your abdomen rise and, as you breathe out slowly, let the breath out with the sensation of calm.

After the fourth breath (and a few more if that helps you), tap into that feeling of inner calm and allow yourself time to be fully present again. This is the experience of quietening the mind and getting back in contact with the peace of your inner self.

Keep practising these breaths throughout your day and notice how you calm down with each one.

Put these four deep breaths into your toolkit. Anytime you experience in any way a feeling of unease — before you go into a meeting, when you are feeling anxious on an aeroplane, before you go into the dentist's surgery, during an intense work meeting — bring yourself back to them. Allow yourself the time to bring about a different sensation.

EXERCISE 4: *Being in the Present Moment*

Starting with two minutes every day, allow your focus to be consciously drawn to the present moment and away from the chatter of the mind. Whether you do this on a journey to work, sitting at home or prior to an evening meal, just give yourself a little time to enjoy being fully present.

This isn't about forcing your mind to be blank, as is often thought; it is about absorbing yourself in what is actually occurring right now. You can move your awareness around your environment, searching out for points of reference that you like — a picture, a flower, a person, the silence, the sounds, the space in between you and objects — and allowing yourself a moment of enjoyment.

The first few times you might like to ask yourself, 'Am I enjoying my point of focus?' just to check you are not focusing on something in the room but still allowing your thoughts to roam around your painful past! If you find you are moving back to fearful thoughts or memories, then use your cancelling statement or four deep breaths to bring your focus back once again. Let yourself be absorbed in what is occurring in the present moment and the feelings of freedom this can bring.

Gradually, as the weeks move on, increase the time of awareness from a few minutes to more and more of your everyday life. Allow yourself the luxury of accepting the gift that is the present.

Chapter 4

Misunderstanding our Possessions, Desires and Ownership:
Diverting Away from Attachment

The greatest of all enemies of man is himself.

—*PARAMAHANSA YOGANANDA*

How do you view life? Is it a constant struggle? Are you weighed down by the day-to-day humdrum? When do you allow yourself the space to really enjoy living, and to experience something new?

We do have the power to do things in a completely new way. But that means taking responsibility for our life, and this can feel quite difficult. Many of us have found a million and one ways to avoid it. Attachment is one of them.

Attachment is often thought of as being attached to the external world, material objects and 'stuff'. But attachments to emotional ties, beliefs or ways of being can also reinforce our lack of fulfilment. So, how can we divert away from attachment and live in harmony with what we have and who we are right now?

'WHAT I DESIRE...'

The word 'desire' has confused many people, including me at times. Yes, it can mean a sexual urge, or wanting a physical object or experience, and some people think that the fulfilment of such desires will never lead to happiness. Yet you can also desire happiness, love and peace, so can desire be all bad? If we can understand where our desires are coming from and how they can change, we will understand far more about how to reclaim happiness.

When I was younger, whilst studying and embracing the first steps of this path I had jobs in many weird and wonderful places, from pharmaceutical, toy and smoked salmon factories (the last one didn't last long) to shoe shops and pubs. If I'd got through the days thinking, 'I'm stuck here and that's it,' I wouldn't be where I am today. I'm not actually helping people *more* now than when I was packing breakfast cereals, just doing it in a different way. But that way resonates with how I am today and it has been the desire to find real inner happiness that has led me forward. Learning to move forward without being totally attached to the desire and allowing the experience of my inner self was a good first step.

Swami Pabhavananda and Christopher Isherwood's commentary on attachment has always brought me great understanding. Their teachings explain that if we are only going to try and control the negative thought waves of desire without raising waves of love, compassion and devotion to oppose them, then we will just become agitated and unbalanced. If we are trying not to think 'bad' thoughts, we can easily fail, and the subsequent humiliation can be overwhelming. Why go through all that when you can find peace and happiness comfortably through simple questioning and observation? Let the questions in this section be a starting-point to addressing your own attachments and desires, not to block them out, but to let in greater self-love and compassion.

LEARNING ALL THE WAY

We are all learning in life, but our experiences and challenges can be so very different. I believe that we choose the conditions we are born into in order to experience what we need to in this life. We can become so attached to these conditions, however, that even if they are traumatic, we can cling to them rather than choose happiness. Or we may feel that life has thrown something at us and we just have to accept it. So, for example, we may try to uphold the idea that it is OK to have a relationship where our partner does not treat us well, or that it's natural to struggle, or that poor health is our lot because it runs in the family.

People have often tried to convince me that we should lower our expectations of life so that we aren't disappointed. The idea is that it is safer to not reach for the stars in case we end up in the gutter. But then we will always feel lack, whereas imagining the ultimate in happiness means that we are allowing it to be a possibility. And that will be enough to start the process of attracting it.

If you find yourself attached to a specific way of being or tradition that does not resonate with your own happiness, then you can start to attract that happiness by embracing a slightly different method of living your life. We can be attached to certain traditions by fear or emotional pressure, and this can be paralyzing, but if you feel in your heart that you could find happiness by choosing a new way of life, try it.

'Nicola, it's not that easy — you don't know my family' is the usually the response when I suggest this. OK, I may not personally know your family, but I can understand that they think their way is right for you. And I know that you can feel a deeper love towards your family when you are at peace within yourself rather than when you are living a life that does not resonate with you. You will all benefit from this. So, if love is what you want to feel, find the right way for you to feel it and the gift will be shared.

THANK YOU

I have heard from countless clients about financial burdens, and I have also let them become major influences on my own life at times. I remember taking out a loan to start up my own psychology practice. I had never had a loan before and it felt pretty huge to say the least. But I was able to avoid being weighed down by it by choosing to view it as a gift. I was grateful for it and within four years it was paid back.

How emotionally tied are you to your financial situation? I have heard clients talk about being 'shackled' to their debts. I have seen clients who are so scared of losing money they won't have a joint account with their spouse, clients who won't allow themselves to spend any of their money on enjoying life and clients who live in fear of never having enough, even though they actually do have enough. Money is such a wonderful topic to explore, precisely because it elicits such strong responses.

It is understandable that when you have a mortgage, you are concerned about borrowing a huge sum of money and having to pay it back. But why not enjoy your new home a little more by lifting the emotional burden? And how about thanking the bank for lending you the money for your home?

As for renting, it is amazing that so many people see it as throwing money away. I see it as the perfect exchange: here you are giving me a beautiful space to live in and here I am giving you some money.

What did your parents teach you about money? Will there never be enough? Will it always go out as soon as it comes in? Will it make you happy? Will it bring you freedom? Will it even matter at all?

Take a moment to think how your relationship with money has been shaped by your parents' relationship with money.

- What are your own beliefs about money?
- How do you maintain these beliefs? Do you hoard your belongings in case you can't afford to replace them, or criticize others' frivolous relationship with money? Or are you always saving in case of an emergency? Or spending uncontrollably, for it is your right to do so?
- How influenced are you by others' expectations of how much money you should have?

- How much are your fears about money related to fears of not feeling secure or safe enough?
- How does having money separate you from other people?
- Do you consider yourself more or less successful when you have more or less money?

If you have realized that you have some limiting patterns concerning money, now is the time to add an appropriate affirmation to your list:

'I love being able to save money with ease.'
'I allow money to flow into my life, always knowing that I have enough.'
'I love developing a harmonious relationship with having, saving and spending money.'

You can also send out a message of gratitude to the universe. Focus on what it is you are actually grateful for — your beautiful home, wonderful neighbours, holiday, car — and appreciate the wonder of it. Gratitude brings recognition of what has already shown up in your life.

It is a big shift from feeling you don't have enough to appreciating what you do have and understanding that it is enough. Cancelling any snowballing thoughts about lack of money and taking a few deep breaths before opening bills is a great start. Give yourself permission to see the truth of your situation and then you can open yourself up to improving it. Why go through life with fear and dread when comfort and clarity are also possible?

How easy it is to look at where we are and want to have something better. But if we are grateful for what we have, it is as if we are welcoming in even more by saying thank you in advance. Gratitude welcomes in the new. Right now, could you find one aspect of the here and now to be grateful for?

Considering that you are taking the steps, in your own comfortable way, towards making each day better in your life, why not thank yourself too? How often have you said to yourself, 'I'm actually doing OK and I'm glad to be me. I'm grateful for who I am'? OK, well in that case you'd better start!

ATTACHMENT AND RELEASE

Our attachment to specific ideas and beliefs can also prevent us from reclaiming happiness. We can become so attached to them that we don't open ourselves up to the possibility of things happening any other way. We may be asking for change, but are we standing there with open arms to actually embrace it?

Take a moment and think about how you would feel if everything that you are asking to experience were to show up today — the love of your life, the perfect job, the financial security, the plane ticket to travel, your own business, true peace and love… How would you feel? Most people say, 'Grateful!' Then, moments later, they realize that in order to embrace these things they would have to let go of closely held attachments.

Let's address the eight common attachments and look at how we can divert ourselves away from them. For each of these attachments, allow yourself to think of at least one time in your life when you experienced the consequences of focusing on this limiting idea.

1. Attached to the Lack

When the universe doesn't appear to be bringing what we want, we can become fully focused on the lack of it. We can become consumed by what we *don't* have.

To gain an idea of how useful this approach is, next time you are in the company of someone who wants to experience something else in their life, listen to their language, their descriptions of themselves and how easily they think they can fulfil this desire. Then ask yourself whether the energy of their thoughts matches what they are hoping for.

Some people joke about what they lack, even though it brings them great pain. Clients wishing to lose weight, for example, have reported making horrible jokes about the way they look, even to their loved ones. We should never ever joke about our pain — it doesn't help us or anyone else. We don't need to hurt ourselves in case someone else does first. We are here to nourish ourselves and learn how to let others nourish us too.

We can even define ourselves according to what we lack, describing ourselves as a victim of life, unlucky, always going without. We are obviously lowering our expectations here, and if we do choose to attach our whole identity to where we are now, then we have no way of being open to the new. If, for example, you are going about calling yourself 'the singleton' and reinforcing this with every thought, word and deed, are you going to notice the string of potential partners available? You may have been sitting next to one on your journey to work, but been so busy figuring out how to busy up your evening in order not to feel lonely that you didn't look up and smile at them.

If we are focused on lack, we will attract even more lack — and then we can easily use this to confirm that we are *never* going to have what we want.

So, when we do know what we want, it's important that we don't try and get it by constantly reaffirming that it is *not* there! Reinforce possibility rather than impossibility and lack.

When have you become so focused on what you don't have that you've felt unable to view yourself any other way?

2. Attached to the Outer Experience

We live in a world of great sensory pleasure. It can be all too easy to become attached to this busy outer world at the expense of going within and experiencing a calm peaceful self.

Also, we often feel that if we are in pain, going within will only enhance this. But if we undertake this inner exploration, we can gain so much and experience so much more than we ever expected.

There may be many reasons why we have become attached to our outer experience. Fear is usually one of the main themes. What will I find if I look within myself? Will I like it? Will I be able to cope?

Whatever we may think about ourselves right now, an inward journey will spark a natural evolutionary process towards how we would like to be. Give yourself this chance to grow.

Learning to calm the mind and go within may seem like a foreign concept when you are used to constant mind chatter. I have seen countless different reactions in students who are learning to do this. As they start to relax and move their senses away from external stimuli, some laugh and giggle, others find that their clothing needs constant adjustment, or that it is difficult to close their eyes and keep still, or all too easy to fall asleep. None of these are 'wrong' reactions in any way — just part of the journey. When you are starting out, don't ask too much of yourself, just be where you are. Failing to sit in meditation for an hour on the first day won't reinforce your love of the process. Allow yourself to enjoy each part of the journey, whatever it brings, even if at first that is simply becoming aware of your negative mind chatter. Every part of this is a wonderful step towards something better.

Some people want to remain attached to their outer experience, as they feel that going within means that they will have to 'act spiritual' or 'be good' and it is easier to live without this burden. So know that just being yourself is good enough. And you cannot fail at that because it is all you ever *can* be. Your spiritual path is yours to enjoy in the way that is right for *you*. So do enjoy it.

3. Attached to the Powers Rather than the Truth

On this journey of spirit we can find that the ego creeps in, saying that we have to be the best at it. This can be complicated by the fact that as we open up to the wisdom within, we can gain new abilities — and become attached to them.

Once, during a stage of my life involving deep meditation practice each morning, I found that I became more aware of energies. Seeing colours, lights and moving blobs became quite normal to me. This is the most technical way I can describe this to you!

One night I was woken by my husband snoring (he doesn't usually snore). I went into the lounge and lay down on the cushions (again this is something I never usually do). As I lay down I saw a man. He was as real to me as anyone has ever been, but was what you might call a spirit or ghost.

Initially I was shocked, but my ego had just been waiting for this one and I began to get very attached to the idea that I was psychic. 'Yippee, I'm different, I'm better, look what I can do! Now I need to get really good at it and be the best in the world and then I'll be happy!' I went to workshops and found I could easily pick up techniques. So I developed some huge expectations of the future. None of this made me any happier, though, not one bit.

In no way do I think that having psychic gifts is wrong. They are as natural as any other talent. I am telling you this story because I became so attached to having them that this ultimately this led me off my path of inner fulfilment — for a little while. Eventually, I saw these powers as a gift in themselves and came to accept them much more graciously, without thinking that they made me a better person. I learned much more about myself by being willing to look at how I *was* rather than what I could *do*, and the consequence was that I had no desire to have such experiences again.

Whatever your natural gifts, allow them to flow, but remember that you don't need to prove how special you are. Allow your natural gifts to be accepted without becoming attached to them.

4. Attached to the Struggle

Just as we can become attached to lack, we can become attached to the belief that getting what we want has to be hard. We can become attached to this struggle because it demonstrates that by achieving what we hope for, we are right and therefore others are wrong.

Let's address these points separately. You may already hold the belief that life has to be hard. Take a moment to address what aspects have to be hard — earning money, having stable relationships, achieving your goals, being creative, having time for yourself? They will be as hard as you believe they will be. If you are constantly saying that you have no time, then you will always be faced with the physical reality of situations that match this.

There is a current advertisement for identity theft on many of my train journeys. It states that 'at least seven people in this carriage' are going to be victims of identity theft. I always see this and then say to myself that I am not one of those seven. My life does not have to be a struggle.

Now, looking at the struggle in terms of proving you are right — why do you *need* to be right? Why do you need to prove that your way was worth the struggle and pain? I can't emphasize this enough: your way is your way, but it doesn't have to be the *only* way. If you feel that others' ideas have held you back from being happy, you don't need to prove them incorrect in order to be happy. Just be happy.

One final point: there are certain perspectives that teach that life is a struggle and our suffering is important. However, do you need to suffer in order to be happy?

5. Attached to the Physical

How would you describe your physical body? Has it let you down? Does it look the way you want it to? Why does this matter so much?

We are fed body-shape stereotypes and new ways to achieve them every day. Do these make you feel happy or inadequate? If despair and self-criticism start to snowball when you look in the mirror, remember you can stop them before they take over. Embrace what you are and give yourself a kind thought right away. Let every day be full of total self-love rather than habitual self-loathing.

So often we use our physical body as a means of demonstrating our ability to control: maintaining exercises, diets and other regimes, and probably becoming obsessed with the ageing process as well. This will never bring us peace, whereas learning to accept and embrace the cycle of our life can be the most freeing experience. We learn to enjoy where we are right now without fearing the next stage won't be as good or not fully embracing this one because we feel that the next one will be even better. Why give up loving yourself now?

Another way of learning to become content with our body is to address our view of pleasure and pain. We can become attached to both. Do you feel that you have to push your body to the limit in order to feel pleasure? Do you feel that you only know your body when it is showing you pain? How about just loving and respecting the wonderful being that you are, whatever is happening to your body? Give yourself the gift of seeing your body as an incredible vehicle for an incredible you. As you learn to enjoy being in your body, your awareness can shift to seeing it as a gift rather than an unfulfilling burden.

6. Attached to It Being our Way

Life unfolds in its own way and the more we learn and experience, the greater our capacity to love and give. However, we can become attached to such a rigid picture of how life *should* unfold that we forget to open the space for it to arrive.

Many people put age restrictions and milestones in place and then feel the internal pressure to live up to these deadlines. But life is so different for each of us, how can we possibly compare the stages? And following other people's rigid patterns will mean sometimes ignoring our own wishes. So, rather than put pressure on yourself, why not choose to embrace the opportunities that are actually arising for you, even if they aren't coming in the exact format that you have prescribed?

Often when life doesn't work out as we have anticipated, we feel we have failed. Where do you feel that you have failed? What pressure have you put on yourself for things to turn out one specific way? Remember you cannot possibly fail at life, as it is not a succeed or fail situation. It is an *experience* and you are experiencing it. That's all good.

Sometimes we can let one 'failure' stop us from continuing this journey of change. Clients often get frustrated and angry when they reach a point of challenge, but working through challenges is all part of the journey. At such times, if we can stand back and observe what is happening, we may just get a glimpse that something great is on its way, only not wrapped up in the form that we expected. We may still be moving forward, but perhaps on a wider path in different shoes.

Success can come in many guises. Stay open to the possibility. Most of all, stay open to it being different from what you are expecting.

7. Attached to How Others Must Be

I love the quote by Sir Boyle Roche, 'Disappointment is the nurse of wisdom.' As well as being disappointed that life hasn't brought what we wanted, we can feel that a *person* has not produced what we wanted.

A therapist once told me a joke about a client who said that they didn't have any issues. The therapist asked them to telephone their family and then get back to them for an appointment.

We have a great deal to learn from our families, friends and acquaintances. And we can become very attached to ideas of how they ought to behave! When they don't behave in this way, deep love can mix with deep disappointment. They did not live up to their role. They did not do what they were meant to do. They did not care for us as we wanted.

As we work towards a greater feeling of ease within ourselves, we can begin to step away from the pain and see our loved ones in a new way. It will help if we give ourselves permission to feel whatever we need to in order to move through the pain. Many clients, for example, hold in their feelings of anger towards their parents so that they do not appear to be bad children. They are *not* bad children — just people who are working through their attachment to what they wanted their parents to be like.

We can have similar attachments to our friends, neighbours and even colleges, and often get angry, frustrated and impatient with them as a result. When we are very hard on other people it is usually a sign that we are equally hard, if not harder, on ourselves. So let's give ourselves a break and allow others the same luxury.

Whilst addressing our attachment to others, it is also important to address the increase of celebrity culture. This keeps us from focusing our mind away from our incredible true self and believing others are in some way better. I have seen people watch whole television programmes and then comment on how much *better* everyone is than them and how bad it makes them feel. But other people are no better than we are — this is just an illusion that keeps us from our own inner happiness.

If you find yourself around people who in any way ignite a feeling of unworthiness in you, why not try something new? Why not see yourself as they are and tap into how you imagine they are feeling? If you admire your teacher for their capacity to communicate, for instance, why not tap into the feeling of communicating as they do? If you see someone succeeding in a business and aspire to do the same, focus on being that success. Reacting to others can be a gift if you can then connect with the potential within yourself.

8. Attached to the Change Process

When we embark on a period of growth we can become very attached to how it is going to happen. We can literally become attached to learning not to be attached!

The way to divert away from this is to take the pressure off ourselves to be a certain way by a certain time and just allow ourselves to be the way that we are now.

After all, all that anyone can do is — as my wonderful teacher Ernest Coates says — 'try your best and leave the rest'. Perfect!

'I GOTTA HAVE IT'

Have you ever noticed the direct correlation between your mood and wanting to buy something? I know that when I have felt happy I have chosen to have my lunch in the park, whereas when I have felt slightly less happy, I have reached out for retail therapy. I have quite literally watched myself shop for something that I know won't bring me the happiness I am after. So, why am I doing this? Why might you be doing this?

Purchasing and owning can bring a whole mixture of feelings to the surface. How would you describe your feelings when you finally own an item that you have wanted for a while? Happiness? Relief? Guilt? Dissatisfaction as you remind yourself of all of the other things that you don't have? Temporary pleasure? Concern that the item isn't good enough or exactly what you wanted? Joy? Excitement? Confusion as to why you really wanted it in the first place?

This mixture shows us that there is so much more going on here than the simple purchase of things we believe we need. This opens up the question of what we really need to be happy. We can derive short-term satisfaction from buying something, and I am not trying to take that away from you. You deserve it, after all. You are learning to nourish yourself. But the pleasure is often temporary. Isn't it better to nourish yourself by working towards a permanent state of happiness rather than reaching out for a temporary high? Doesn't a temporary high open up the possibility of a temporary low again? With this mindset we just set ourselves up for further inner angst.

Furthermore, we are living in a world with great sensory pleasures, rapid technological growth and a recycling system that cannot cope with our increasing waste.

So allow yourself the luxury of seeing what is actually necessary for your life and what are extra burdens and pressures that do not lighten your load or the load of the planet.

Try this exercise.

EXERCISE 5: '*What Do I Want?*'

Take a moment right now to look at what is presently in your life and ask yourself:

- 'What does this say about me?'
- 'Who am I trying to be?'
- 'What is involved in that?'
- 'Is this enough to make me feel good about myself?'

When you find yourself purchasing from a need to feel better, give yourself a break. You are obviously not feeling at ease, so extra criticism won't help. Take a few deep breaths and allow yourself the gift of no guilt, no burden and no pressure as you come back to that calm feeling. As you come back to that point of calm, you can see when you are reaching out for something that is merely a short-term cover-up of deeper unfulfilment. Then you can continue with your day.

EXERCISE 6: *New Steps Forward*

To give yourself a gentle reminder of how you can move forward, refer to your list of new thought patterns and for each one write down an action you could take to support that. If you are working towards a new job, for example, you could write a CV, have a chat with a careers advisor or search the internet for possible employers. If you are working towards being more self-confident, you could accept an invitation to a gathering or smile at a stranger. If you are hoping to improve your intuition, you could consciously ask yourself each morning, 'What do I feel like doing today?'

You don't have to start with a grand gesture, unless you feel that is right for you — something small will work equally well. Be good to yourself as you make the changes and let these new actions resonate with the words 'comfortable', 'possible' and 'new'. Start by taking just one new action each day.

Chapter 5

Misunderstanding our Anger, Resentment and Blame:
Diverting Away from Pain

You will find as you look back upon your life that the moments when you have truly lived are the moments when you have done things in the spirit of love.

—*HENRY DRUMMOND*

Anger, resentment and blame are important states to understand, for they keep us (and often everyone around us) from love, peace and harmony. I am not suggesting that we stop emotion from flowing here, but it's worth considering how we could direct that energy to find a greater sense of peace.

I often hear that clients don't want to feel anger at all, as they aren't sure they can control it. Children growing up in a violent household can often feel that anger is not a safe emotion to express. Equally, they can grow up believing that it is OK to be angry at everyone and everything. Our beliefs about anger and how it can be expressed can be so diverse. Take a moment to think about how anger is expressed within you. Do you find that you sweat and shake, or want to run away or fight? Without judgement, just look at how you express your internal unease and in what situations.

Once, for a period of three weeks, I suffered the worst acid reflux and digestive pain imaginable. It was so intense that for a week I couldn't lie down properly to sleep — I had to prop myself upright with a pillow. There were three days when I could only eat plain rice and yoghurt — any other food was like digesting a plate of nails. The reason behind it was that I literally could not digest my anger. I was angry with an individual who had caused harm to a loved one and I wouldn't let it go.

Eventually, of course, I realized that my pain wasn't helping me in any way, shape or form. In fact I was sending out such anger into the universe that I was attracting anger back from total strangers. My only way forward was to release what I was storing inside myself as disease.

Once a week, before work, while sitting in my car waiting for the parking restriction to end, I would write a letter to the person I was angry with. I would write down everything in graphic detail — the anger, the injustice, the implications, the pain — until I felt that I had covered everything. Sometimes I would fill five A4 pages. When the letter was written and the parking restriction was over, I would walk past a litter bin, imagine that it was a post box and happily deliver my letter. I would always hold the intention 'Now it is all gone.' Then I would allow myself the luxury of walking away feeling lighter and less angry.

I did this for several weeks. After a month there was less to write. Eventually I would have to sit there and have a good think about why I was angry before I could write anything at all. The point was, I *wasn't* angry anymore.

Please take note that my intention was never to actually send the letter, or to cause harm to anyone — I was learning how to release my anger in order to send love to them. Hurting other people doesn't resolve anger, it simply reinforces internal unrest. My aim was purely to release the anger I was bottling up and reach a point of peace. Before I started the exercise I would reinforce this with both words ('Nicola, this is to bring you to greater ease') and emotion (vital for the buy-in of the subconscious).

If you are feeling angry, think of a way in which you could develop a gentle form of expression for yourself and a time and a place where you could do it. Twenty minutes is all you need. Some people visit a therapist to work through their inner turmoil, while others find that they need quiet reflection. Different situations may call for different responses. Be flexible and know that there are many forms of help available.

The interesting point is that once I didn't need to write anger-releasing letters anymore, I decided to use this time to start reinforcing with gratitude a new state of being for myself, my family and my friends. I would start my new letters with 'Dear Universe' and then write pages of thank yous for what I was creating in my life, even if it hadn't arrived yet: 'Thank you for my perfectly functioning digestive system, thank you for my happy healthy family, thank you for my increasing client base, thank you for my successful career...' I would then deliver my letter into the litter bin/post box and walk away feeling great. Tuning into what you are grateful for in your life in the present moment is a great exercise to do anytime.

My digestive system returned to optimal functioning without any further intervention, I regained my composure and subsequently this was reflected in my life. The most important point here is that by working through my anger, I could see the situation from a wider perspective and, as a result, send out love instead of hatred. Never forget: love heals, anger does not.

I'm not suggesting that my initial anger wasn't helpful in this process. If I hadn't felt it, I wouldn't have learned that love felt so much better! The obvious physical pain was also a gift — a nudge in the right direction. The resonance of disharmony can have profound effects on us. Disharmony in the mind is disharmony in the body.

So what does your current mindset resonate with?

HOW DO YOU SEE YOURSELF?

How we identify ourselves affects how we relate to other people, our environment and our current situation in life. So, how do you see yourself? What mindset do you adopt? And how does this affect your emotions and tendencies to feel frustrated and angry?

The Struggler Mindset

Do you feel that you are struggling with life, that events are out of your control and inflicted upon you? Do you feel as though life is against you?

When do you get angry? When others succeed with an internal strength that you feel you don't have? When they don't treat you with respect? When life seems to be dealing you challenge after challenge while other people seem to breeze through?

The Watcher Mindset

Do you always feel you have to watch everything like a hawk just in case anyone tries to deceive you or beat you or find out about the real you?

When do you get angry? When someone catches you out? When someone betters you or doesn't treat you as well as you think you deserve?

The Disease Mindset

Are you always unwell? Does your life revolve around trying to stay well even when you aren't sick? Does your routine involve trying to fend off future disease rather than embrace perfect health now? Do you know as much pain as pleasure?

When do you get angry? When people with vast emotional resilience don't understand your sensitive pathway? When you are taken out of the rigid regime of diet and exercise that helps you to feel well? When you are forced into pushing your physical or emotional comfort boundaries?

The Helper Mindset

Are you constantly looking after other people? Do you get caught up in everyone else's dramas? Do you always put someone else's needs first? Do you have a moment just to rest, without having to do something with or for someone else?

When do you get angry? When people seem to focus on themselves rather than on helping other people? When they decide to try something new, away from your help? When they take your help but are never there to support you? When they don't need you anymore?

The Saviour Mindset

Do you feel that there is always a positive difference to be made? Does life hold the potential for doing good?

When do you get angry? When others don't care as much as you do? When they focus on accumulation rather than sharing? When they seem to find giving a foreign concept? When no one has the time for anyone else? When others are stuck in their pain and this frustrates you?

The Holder Mindset

Do you feel that you have to hold everything together? That without your special way of doing things life just wouldn't work?

When do you get angry? When others threaten your authority? When they question whether you really know best? When they let you down? When they don't live up to your standards?

The Grafter Mindset

Do you think the good things in life should only go to those who work hard?

When do you get angry? When people have more than you or have it easier than you? When they get the same or better results in an easier way? When they don't work as hard as you?

The Avoider Mindset

Do you feel that you try your best but are a long way from where you want to be? Do you have lots of ideas about what you would love to do but never seem to claim them as your experience in life?

When do you get angry? When other people seem to achieve everything they set out to do? When they question you about the progress of your projects? When you see others doing exactly what you want to be doing in life?

The Lucky Mindset
Do you feel blessed? Do you feel as though life just unfolds and you are ushered through it with support and care?

When do you get angry? When others constantly moan about their lives?

If any of these suggestions resonates with you, think for a moment of how the thoughts that you are sending out are related to these underlying beliefs and how they will match the physical reality of your experience. I cannot reinforce this enough: if every day, every thought and every action is fuelled by the idea that you are sick or downtrodden, this thought energy will gain enough momentum to bring you that exact physical reality. Like attracts like. Watch how you react to others and notice when your mindset is resonating with their pain and you are buying into it with your own frustration. Notice also, how you can easily separate yourself from others.

The good news is that you can change your mindset right now, today.

FREEDOM FROM PAIN

Freedom from pain and suffering is something we all want — that goes without saying. Luckily, in exactly the same way that we can create pain for ourselves, we can also ease our own suffering.

Pain is different for us all, as is our ability to cope with it. This can have a great impact on our change process. If we feel that someone has moved forward more easily than we have, we may get frustrated and angry at ourselves. That won't help us. We all have our own path.

Let us also remind ourselves of the power of our subconscious. We may think that every part of us wants to be free of pain, but we may have numerous files in our subconscious reinforcing why we need to stay in pain. Could you look at your current discomfort and see how it might keep you safe, protected from something that might scare, worry or even unbalance you? As such a great deal of learning happens in childhood, you may not even know. That's fine. You don't need to spend a lifetime digging for answers. The present moment is always the most important one you will ever have.

A very common frustration related to this is that we may feel that we have wasted a whole lifetime. If you ever feel like this, just remember that in the grand scheme of this life, you only ever have *now*.

Not only do people get angry about perceived wasted time, but also about what they were led to believe was necessary in order to find happiness — the good job, the house, the children, the hobbies, the nice car, the membership of prestigious societies… You may have had all these things and still not been happy.

So now what? I'm not suggesting that you throw out your family and belongings and sit in silence. I *am* suggesting that you start with what you have right now. Be grateful for it. This will allow you to see it as the foundation of your inner fulfilment. And if you see someone who is happy, don't be jealous or angry, but watch what they do to maintain that happiness. Then you can work out whether that would be right for you too.

Easing the suffering starts as you move away from past mindsets and towards a present moment that can provide you with the contentment that you are after. Reliving old hurts, past wrong-doing and long-gone incidents will only draw you back to that same suffering that occurred. The only time to embrace a new you is right now, and in this now is the peace of the present. It is a present in itself.

'I HAVE TO BE IN PARADISE'

So many people seem to believe that they have to be somewhere else in order to feel peace and happiness. Where they are right now is never quiet enough, calm enough, still enough, perfect enough. But if you are spending all your time sending out the thought energy that you can't find the peace that you could when you were on holiday and or at that retreat, what do you think you are going to create in your life? A constant lack of peace in the present and a projection that peace will only come in a certain situation in the future.

I have had moments of profound meditation just off one of the busiest roads in central London. I have also sat in a quiet 'paradise' and felt tired, lazy and un-satisfied. That has been my inner journey of learning. It hasn't been to do with my environment, but to do with me. As Swami Niranjanananda Saraswati so perfectly writes, 'There is no peace in the Himalayas, and there is no noise in the world; everything is within you. If you are at peace within yourself, you can find peace anywhere in the world, and if you are not at peace with yourself, you will never find this peace in the isolation of the mountains.'

I have heard so many reasons why people can't find peace in their everyday lives. I have even taught yoga classes in beautiful studios and heard students commenting that other students were preventing them from relaxing because they were breathing too loudly (yes, really), scratching or wobbling too much. These real examples show that when our focus in not within and centred, we can manage to be annoyed by *anything*. We literally throw away the joy of the present moment because of our own unease and anxiety. On the other hand, I have taught students in situations where the noise outside the room has been so loud that I have had to shout and yet have still watched students move into the deepest states of relaxation and meditation. What is possible in one situation is possible in another. You just have to allow yourself to move away from the assumption that it is not.

You don't need to step onto the stress train just because that is what you believe a situation calls for. You can happily walk down a calmer path, and that energy will then affect your whole being, others in your environment and your whole life.

So think for a moment:

- When do you find that you blame your *situation* for your state of being?
- When do you blame *others* for your state of being?

Looking at how you react now will enable you to move towards peace.

And remember, at those moments when you become focused on someone doing something that irritates you, those deep breaths are ready and waiting, along with the reinforcement: 'I am calm, at peace and totally relaxed in myself.'

Learning to observe your own angst will shine a light on the real power that you have to choose something different.

STAYING AWAY

Staying away from others may actually seem a good way to find peace, but ultimately this will not help us, as it means we can't benefit from the help they can give. I am not suggesting that we opt for telling the whole world about our problems and reinforcing them with every word. I am suggesting that we reach out for the support that we deserve.

There may be a whole barrel full of excuses why we don't do this: we are a private person, no one can help us, we're a lost cause, we're too damaged, we want to keep this within the family, we're embarrassed… These beliefs and this egoic mindset don't help us, they only seal us off from the help that is available to us. But the moment we change our belief to 'I am open to letting in help', we will find ourselves supported in more ways than we imagine.

What about other excuses for not seeking help? Money always seems to be a big one. If you don't have enough money to spend on finding a practitioner to help you, what about diverting the money you spend on clothes, shoes, nights out and so on to finding peace, health and happiness? If you still don't have enough money, check out teaching hospitals or alternative and complementary health courses and schools. These rely on their students practising on real people, and prices are low and supervision immense. Don't believe that these students 'won't be as good' as other practitioners — remain positive and that way you will attract someone who is good.

Another idea is to call someone up, explain you need their help but cannot afford the full payment and ask whether they can recommend where to go or can see you for less. I get asked this frequently myself and so far I have always been able to give suitable advice or direction.

Time is another interesting excuse. We often don't feel that we have enough time as it is and taking on something else would be a burden. If you feel like this, just set aside 20 minutes every day to relax, read this book and tune into your new positive thoughts. You could even do it on a journey into work. Start by structuring in a space in every day to dedicate to your own needs. This can grow. Of course, what I really mean is to stop buying into and living out your belief that the present moment cannot be one of peace. You can at any stage of your day choose to put your focus on a few calming breaths, or move your mind away from the continual swirling of fearful thoughts. The idea that time is the factor that stops you from feeling calm seems irrelevant when at any time you need nothing more than to change your focus to experience greater peace.

THE TRUTH APPEARS AFTER THE ANGER

What happens within you when you encounter a situation which makes you angry? Do you want to shout and scream or do you hold it all in? Do you want to fight or do you feel paralyzed? Do you want to stand your ground or run away?

Being angry often masks the truth of a situation. But if we can focus on those four deep, slow, smooth breaths and calm ourselves down, the angry smokescreen will dissipate and we will be able to understand what is really happening around us.

Something that may come to light is the real reason for our anger. By being angry, are we maintaining the position that another person is wrong? Does holding onto our anger prove to the world that we are a good person? Or that we have something important to say? Does it actually feel so natural to be angry that we can't imagine feeling any other way? Are we angry with ourselves for what we have done to others?

We are here to love and cherish each other, but sometimes we bump into others on our path through life. At times our actions may hurt others and theirs may hurt us. So give yourself permission to learn from any times when you hurt others, and grow towards a more peaceful present and future, without guilt. Choose happiness and work towards it right now.

WHERE YOU PLACE YOURSELF

Do you seem to find yourself in situations that don't resonate with peace and happiness? Do you hang out in violence-prone pubs and clubs? Or take part in debating groups that are fuelled with anger rather than insight? Or keep company with volatile friends and acquaintances?

Many people try to find peace while maintaining connections with groups and activities that resonate with unease! The reasons for these choices may be linked to various patterns and beliefs. What is of vital importance, however, is to do activities that make us feel good. We may have to throw out some preconceptions on the way, of course. I thought that yoga was for old hippies until I actually tried it! We can block off whole areas of life by not being open to them.

You may feel that your current friends or family will ridicule you for trying something new. Remember that if this is the case, they have their own reasons for not changing, but that's no reason for *you* not to change. Your life may involve watching others staying in their own suffering while you move towards a life of greater peace. If the people in your life don't serve your highest good, welcome in new people. A better experience of life is out there right now — embrace it. You deserve it!

CHALLENGES ALONG THE WAY

If you have experienced moments of happiness, then you know it is possible. Build on those. If you have experienced moments of peace, build on those also. If you have only ever felt anxious, use that as a guide to how you *don't* want to feel and explore some new feelings.

Stand back and observe yourself along the way. Are you feeling more at ease with yourself or constantly comparing yourself to others? Are you jealous of another person's advantages, possessions or even luck? 'Harry doesn't know how lucky he is!' 'It's alright for Claire, but I didn't get the start in life she did.' 'Ryan! *He* seems to get everything he wants.' Just listen to these words. Quite literally you are sending out the message that others get what they want, but you don't. So what sort of energy do you think will match up with these thoughts?

If your mindset says, 'I must fight, I must defend, I must attack to stay safe,' then what is that mindset maintaining? The fear, the concern, the terror that will hold you in this place of anger and violence. It's a vicious circle. Time to break it!

Many of us do feel a point of change calling out within us. And yet we can spend time — even whole lifetimes — resisting it and feeling even more frustrated and angry. But we are not here to be suffocated by internal conflict. Let's move on. How about taking those breaths, working through those affirmations, becoming more observant of your present state, answering these gentle questions and taking a few new actions on the path to happiness?

Often I hear people saying they are frustrated because their prayers aren't being answered or that they have asked and asked for help but nothing is happening. If you feel like this, consider the thought energy of frustration that you are putting out. If, on the other hand, you give yourself the chance to breathe deeply and connect with a feeling of happiness, then you open up the gateway for this to be matched in the world around you. If you are relying on a good future to pull you through, you will be in a state of continual yearning for something different that will never come. Reclaiming something means making that connection now.

'YOU HAVE TO KNOW EXACTLY WHAT I NEED'

Even as we start to acknowledge that we are one part of humanity and that our part fits perfectly into place, we often still have the desire to be understood by others. The pressure we put them under can be immensely high. We expect a response of love, care, support, time and patience, and when they do not (or possibly cannot) give this to us we become frustrated, angry, even bitter.

Here are seven possible scenarios to consider at these times:

1. Are we communicating what we really need from others? 'I really need you to hold me,' 'I really need you to listen to me,' 'I really need you to give me some space to work this situation out,' 'I really need you to help me…'
2. Does showing emotions feel scary, inappropriate, wrong or even bad? Are we able to show what we really feel?
3. Have we already decided what it is that we want to hear from the other person? If they don't give us that, are they wrong? Can others really give their own opinions?

4. If they don't reinforce how bad things are for us, is this frustrating? Is it comforting when others buy into our pain?

5. Are we allowing ourselves to be fully open to help or advice, even if it is different from what we already know can help?

6. Have we restricted another person's help by feeling that they may not be capable of giving us exactly what we want?

7. Are we so low that we don't really believe that anyone can help us, no matter what they say?

When we are in need of help, it is important to let it in. It is safe to show that we have emotions — no one believes that we do not. And it is OK to let others tell us about their experiences — they may show us a way forward. We may feel we know how our life is going to work out, but in truth we don't even know what will happen a week on Wednesday, and that's OK.

It is also OK to seek advice from people other than the ones that you feel you ought to turn to. Use your own feelings to find the right people. And let them in with their advice, help and love.

Others can affect us in many ways — and vice versa. At certain times when we feel frustrated in ourselves, whoever gets in the way can be in the firing line of our frustration. On the other hand, we can walk in on another's anger and be in the firing line ourselves. At these times, think about whether you would prefer to let yourself be drawn into another person's drama or to stay centred within yourself. It can be very easy to blame others for treating us unfairly or drawing us out of our state of calm. But did they take us out of it or did we allow it to happen?

Learning to step back and let others live out their own moments of anger can be very useful. My wonderful husband knows when to leave me in moments of frustration (he may call it 'irrationality') and also knows when we are both open to listening. When he leaves me be, I have to work through my own feelings and I always feel better afterwards. I'm not suggesting that in these moments I don't feel any inner discomfort — of course I do. However, he is giving me the gift of making a change to how I feel and that is one that is treasured. Also, by staying centred and calm within himself, he is giving me permission to do the same. The space is open. I change. I go back to a feeling of connection and love.

We can take this lesson into every area of our life. Say you go on holiday and feel great, then go back to work and on the first day go back to being that old stressed you. Now you have proved that you *can* be calm, and you didn't leave your breathing in left luggage and you most certainly didn't store your awareness away with your suitcase, so why can't you have that feeling now?

I can already hear you telling me that the demands of your job are so great that you aren't able to stay calm. OK, you may have a demanding job, but you may also have accepted that stress is normal because everyone around you is stressed. Have you considered that instead of buying into that, you could be showing them how to do it differently?

When you allow yourself to experience life from a more centred place, you allow the people that are interacting with you to do the same. If you can speak calmly, you make an angry or anxious reaction from another person almost inappropriate. So, if you'd like to become a positive influence on yourself and others, start within. Whenever you feel yourself becoming less centred, breathe out the anxiety and regain a state of calm. Then you can fill up your workplace or home with that holiday feeling!

The challenge here is that in certain situations others may wish that you were angry in order to buy into their mindset. But you know now that accepting that anger won't help you, them or what you are trying to achieve.

When I teach, people are often late, rushed and panicked. They charge into a peaceful session and are a ball of frustration. If I were to buy into this, what would happen? I would feel the same frustration and that would affect me, the other students and how I communicated to the class. So I give the person love, let them settle and within minutes they are calm and centred.

It is amazing how when you start to live from a calm place, you allow each and every interaction with other people to be the same. This is another way of taking responsibility for your own learning and growth. You don't need big gestures if they don't feel right. All you need do is work on the love and peace within yourself and that will have an effect on the rest of humanity.

'I WOULDN'T DO THAT!'

During the time that I was very angry, it was amazing how it came out in my driving. I was so frustrated, I had little patience for other drivers, and guess what was mirrored back? Exactly the same. What made me stop in my tracks was when someone swore at me. I saw what anger looked like and I realized that I didn't enjoy it. It really was that simple.

Sometimes we need to reach a certain point before we are willing to look at our own behaviour. The fact that you are even reading this book says that you are there. So what is your mindset when you are driving? How do other drivers treat you? Are the roads that you turn down always blocked? Be aware of the experiences that you are creating for yourself and the mindset that fuels these.

Always look at yourself and learn with love, rather than criticizing yourself. If you realize you are acting in a way you don't like, that's OK, as now you are doing something to change. And that's another reason for a pat on the back.

EXERCISE 7: *More Awareness, Please*

One way of understanding how you are behaving is to watch the words that you use to describe yourself:

- Are they loving or not?
- What restrictions are there on the free flow of your centred self?
- When do you belittle yourself and when are you kind and loving?
- When do you lose your composure and what do you say about yourself?
- How do you find yourself reacting to others who are angry, stressed or anxious? How do you describe them?
- How easily do you get drawn into their dramas and engage in negative reinforcing conversation?
- How easy it is for you to walk away from situations that are not resonating with peace?
- What activities let you tap into relaxation?
- Do you see how when you feel angry, tense and stressed, others mirror back this to you?

'I CAN'T LET IT GO'

Are you still holding on to something from the past? We can hold onto resentment for days, years, lifetimes even, believing that in some capacity it serves us. But how can we expect to reclaim happiness if every new effort is affected by a half-digested issue that we won't let go of?

Life can bring great trauma, challenges and suffering, of course, and we need to acknowledge our suffering and only move forward in a way that is comfortable for us. Being fully present a little more each day will draw us away from our pain, as will being open to seeing the bigger picture in any way that feels right for us.

'I'M SORRY'

Seeing the bigger picture will also help us move towards an understanding of why forgiveness is important. Forgiveness frees us up; it enables us to find acceptance and understanding. It also sends out the message that we are ready to embrace something new. And when we move towards forgiving ourselves and others, we move towards seeing the world as a kind and loving place.

I say 'move towards' forgiveness because I understand that this is a process just like any other. If I were to say to you that I wanted you to forgive everyone every wrong-doing right now, what would happen? What would your response be? OK, now you get my point.

Forgiveness will become easier if we follow these four steps and work through the following exercise.

1. Acknowledgement
2. Release
3. Love and compassion
4. Peace

EXERCISE 8: *Forgiveness*

Bring to mind a situation about which you feel upset or angry, or even jealous or resentful. Then, with at least ten minutes of quiet, warm space and time, settle yourself down and close your eyes.

Start off by allowing yourself to acknowledge the anger or resentment that you wish to dissolve. Know that it is OK to feel what you feel. You may notice that your mind goes back to a moment of focusing on why you are upset. Again, know that this is OK and just allow yourself to be where you are right now.

Notice how strong the pull to stay with this feeling is. Notice how your mind can search out for other situations of a similar nature to justify your anger. Give yourself the time to feel what you need to — you are learning about your tendencies to stay in discomfort.

Now, as you feel yourself being drawn into the possibility of further negative emotions, I would like you to take eight of those deep, slow, calming breaths.

Imagine that you are halfway down a corridor. At one end is anger; at the other, love and peace. Stand in the middle and just be aware of the choice. See the consequences of both ends — what the pathway to anger could lead to; what the pathway to love could lead to. Take a moment to observe the possibilities.

With this understanding, just feel that you can release the pull towards the anger. Affirm, 'I am now completely releasing any need to feel angry.' Say this a few times with deep emotional investment and start to turn down the corridor towards love.

As you walk down this corridor, imagine that with each step you allow in a greater feeling of love and compassion. Walk at a pace that is comfortable and notice a lightness with each step.

As you look at the walls of the corridor, notice how bright and inviting they are. See them filled with pictures that please and calm you.

When you are nearly at the end of the corridor, take a quick look back and see how far you've come. Feel how good it is to be lighter and calmer.

When you reach the end of the tunnel, notice how you step directly into a space of complete comfort. Stay here for a while enjoying this sensation that you have created, staying present to the gift you have given yourself.

The more you use this technique, the easier it will become. With time and practice, you'll be able to call upon this feeling of peace whenever you need it.

Now cast your mind back to the list you made in Chapter 1. If you remember, I asked you to make a note of any of the suggestions that you felt were coming from outside influences. Look at them again and if any of these cause you any irritation, annoyance or anger, then use this technique to move away from these restrictive feelings.

Forgiveness is your key to freedom.

Chapter 6

Misunderstanding our Self-Love:
Diverting Away from Resistance

There is a light that shines beyond all things on earth, beyond us all,
beyond the heavens, beyond the highest, the very highest heavens.
This is the light that shines in our heart.

— *CHANDOGYA UPANISHAD*

In order to reclaim true happiness we need to divert away from any resistance we may have to it. Resistance can be expressed in a multitude of ways. We may find that we change the conversation every time a certain topic comes up. Or that just when we're on the verge of having a much-needed early night, we always seem to busy ourselves up. Do you find that just when you are about to sit down and actually write that CV, join that gym and/or sign up to that dating agency, you seem to need another drink, some food, to make a phone call, and so on? More than this, we can hold ourselves in work that doesn't fulfil us and relationships that don't nurture us.

Why do we encounter resistance? Surely we all want to be happy?

The problem is that if we are unwilling to accept that we are good enough or worthy enough, then we won't feel that we deserve to be happy. If we don't like who we are, we won't really believe we're good enough to experience our dreams.

We may cite many reasons for not loving ourselves. We may confuse loving or even liking ourselves with narcissistic self-admiration. This is no more than a learned idea that is holding us back.

More often we lack self-love due to past experiences and modelled behaviour. But if we don't love ourselves, we are also losing our connection to the deeper elements of the self. If you don't like what you know about yourself today, will you want to delve deeper?

So, do you love yourself at all? Take some time to reflect on your current feelings. What do you feel about yourself when:

- you look in the mirror?
- you look at your life?

- you look at your relationships?
- you look at other people in your life?
- you look at people you truly admire?

Remember that you are no different from those you admire, although you may believe you are. You are not unworthy, and you are definitely no less deserving than anyone else of experiencing peace and happiness. Now.

'I'M OK JUST AS I AM, THANK YOU!'

Think of something that you have never done but always wanted to, something that would bring you a feeling of fulfilment.

Now ask yourself, 'Why haven't I done this?'

Take a moment to come up with just one reason that you use to justify not embracing something that you actually would like to do. It may be because it would cost money, you have other priorities, other people wouldn't understand, you wouldn't want to do it on your own, it's not the right time, people like you don't do these things, it's not that important after all, you wouldn't want to fail, you wouldn't want to make a fool of yourself… Have I covered it yet?

Let's look at why such a mixed barrel of emotions arises when it comes to fulfilling our hopes and dreams and ultimately enjoying life. Sometimes we don't know what we want, or we do know but don't say anything in case by acknowledging it we have to do something about it. It can feel a lot safer to stay unfulfilled than step up to be happy.

In avoiding happiness, we can use many misunderstandings of what life is about. These may include accumulating more, needing success, and striving to get what we think we should have and do what we feel we should do.

You may have been taught that life should be lived a certain way. That you work to earn money and have hobbies for fun. That to get through it you have to get your head down and work hard. Even that people like you don't succeed in life. I am asking you right now to lose these restrictive and limiting mindsets and choose a new way of being. Listen to what you would really like to do and give yourself permission to actually experience it.

WHAT YOU PUSH DOWN WILL COME UP

Watch young children cry and scream when they first learn that they can't have something that they really want. It doesn't make sense to them because they have yet to develop an understanding of why fun at the park has to stop. As adults, however, we may say 'no' to our own happiness. When we do this, a part of us feels that life isn't fair, but we just get used to this feeling of dissatisfaction and lack and presume it is us. It is not us — it is a feeling of unease.

This inner conflict can remain unresolved for years. And during this time it is amazing how much resentment we can feel towards people who seem to be doing what we want to be doing. Or how frustrated we can feel when we think others are stopping us. We can even let other people's fears get in our way and then feel immense resentment towards those people.

Sometimes we choose the resistant mindset that we have to suffer for what we want — through lack of money, lack of time, lack of peace or lack of love. It is common for people to be doing what they feel is right for them but getting so stressed over it that they aren't actually enjoying it, or to be highly successful in one area and justifying why another area can't be a success — a great career means they can't find love, or their great social life means their health must suffer. But it is possible to enjoy every aspect of life in balance and harmony. Giving up the idea that it has to involve a sacrifice or be a constant strain is a good start.

Go back to what you learned when you observed the words that you used to describe yourself and your world. How many of them were directed towards life being hard? These words are the expressions of your beliefs and I'm sure by now you are getting the idea of how this works. If you hold beliefs that resonate with life being good, what will happen?

If you feel that there is any concern, fear, worry or excuse that you could use in order not to be peaceful and happy, then please go back to your list of affirmations and add in a kind and nurturing statement to support your growth by releasing any patterns of resistance.

WE HAVE TO DO IT

In the previous chapter, we looked at the idea of blame. One of easiest ways to divert away from this is to take responsibility for our own life. If we find ourselves constantly assigning responsibility to others for where we are now, we are saying we can't do anything about it. If we find that we are using others as a reason not to move forward and then resenting them for it, we are choosing to send them our frustration instead of our love. If we take decisions for ourselves, we are saying, 'Yes, I am open to new experiences.'

Others may not understand our learning in life and that's OK, they don't need to, but if we can take responsibility for creating a new state of being within ourselves, we will allow them to see a very different side of us — a side that is capable of giving more love, support and kindness than ever, because we are happier within ourselves.

If you find yourself dwelling on the pain of the past, or on the actions of others in your past, allow yourself to choose a different focus. You aren't denying what happened or suggesting it isn't important, you are just learning from the experience. And as you lose the strength of your attachment to the past, the wounds can begin to heal in the new focus of our present.

Let love fill up the space where pain once lived.

A NEW FEELING

When we have reached a new point of growth, this may result in producing an actual material item, such as this book, or a beautiful garden, or an exam pass. But the most important outcome is the change in our *feelings* — we feel proud, happy, fulfilled, joyful and grateful.

Think of some times in your life when you have felt these feelings. They are wonderful to experience, even if they only last for a short time. So we can become very attached to doing more and more in order to have them again. This can result in a workaholic mindset. So it is worth staying open to the idea that we can feel fulfilled by tapping into our unlimited supply of joy within rather than only by doing or achieving.

Slowly, as we feel more comfortable within, we can experience moments of joy and calm and peace just by being ourselves. And when we do, the world around us mirrors that same beautiful state of just being. Certain days I would walk down roads near work and everyone would smile at me and I would smile back, and strangers would say hello. To be honest, there were a few days when I thought that maybe I had a bit of my lunch hanging off my chin, because I seemed to be drawing such warm and friendly responses there had to be a reason for it. There *was* a reason for it — it was because I was walking around being content and loving and so my world was mirroring this back.

Just to dispel the idea that this can only happen in friendly little towns, I was in central London when I first became aware of this. If you hold the idea that certain places hold powerful potential for love whereas others do not, you are not letting yourself embrace a whole world of possibilities.

If you would like to test this out, think of two places: one where you are always relaxed and happy and one where you are always more stressed and hurried. What do you experience in these places? Why not allow yourself to be that relaxed person today, wherever you find yourself, and see what happens?

STOP, IN THE NAME OF LOVE!

In the previous chapter we began to address the limiting ideas that we don't have enough money or time. Both of these feature highly on the list of why we resist loving and nurturing ourselves.

How could we change our beliefs about money to attract a more harmonious and plentiful experience of it? Could simply observing our spending enable us to see ways to make our life easier? Could we lose the fear that if we spent money on ourselves it would run out?

Every time you make money a reason for not helping yourself, just come back to the idea that you deserve to be helped in every way. So, let today be the day you move towards whatever help you need. Remember, the word 'help' means making something easier for yourself. That is exactly what you are after: making life as easy as it can be. Don't complicate the process by resisting it.

One problem here is that we have accepted stress as normal. It is *not* normal and the more that we accept it is, the longer we will bind ourselves to a life that doesn't provide us with the harmony that we crave. So if you feel under stress, look at how you can relieve that. If you can see a new way of doing something, why not do it? If you feel so weighed down that you can't take on anything else, why not take a few of these pressures away? If all your colleagues feel that working ten hours non-stop in the office is normal, then that is wonderful for them. This is about *you*.

Rejuvenation, replenishment and restoration of our whole being are important. Physically, we were not created to live in a permanent state of stress or anxiety. Moderation and balance are vital in maintaining a well-functioning system. How much of your life is spent running around and how much resting? Are these in balance? What could you do to build in more time for relaxing?

I'm not suggesting that relaxation comes only through passive rest. You may find that going for a walk or swim or reading a book is relaxing for you. Notice how activities you find relaxing ignite that feeling of being connected and doing what is right for you.

Whatever your situation in life, you can find a small amount of space for yourself. You may actually have that space available now, but not be claiming it as your own. I have seen so many adults, particularly parents, give all of their time away and neglect their own health — physical and emotional — in the process. I see people piece themselves together every day, with no regard for their own being, for the sake of their family, job or achievements. What are they modelling to their children about adulthood, parenthood, and life? That it's all fun and then turns into a barrel full of responsibility and pain. If this is you, this is not a time for guilt, this is a time for remembering just how important you are! You deserve to be loved and cared for. Try taking just one hour a week — that is only 60 minutes — to do something for yourself.

'OTHERS NEED ME...'

A very effective technique for deflecting ourselves from loving and helping ourselves is absorbing ourselves in the dramas of others. My years of psychological training have led me to scientifically term this the 'Bob has a broken leg, so I shouldn't moan about my paper cut' syndrome (no offence to all of you Roberts).

In a way, we can be grateful to Bob for having a broken leg. He helps us to tell ourselves that his problems are much worse than ours. We can rally round him, constantly feeling sorry for him, joining him in his suffering and trying to think up ways to help him when we are not even in his company and he needs no more of our focus. We can reinforce the pain and inconvenience the broken leg has brought him by telling him how bad it is and relating numerous stories of broken legs and horrific accidents. By doing this we are actually not helping Bob, but keeping our mind fixed on even more suffering, which may be a familiar place for us. In fact we can even start to fear that we will break our own leg and add that fear to the pile of other fears we are avoiding dealing with. So thank you, Bob, you are helping us in so many ways not to change.

When Bob's leg gets better, we can move on to help Rita and her bad shoulder, so you see we really are far too in demand to ever address our own inner unease...

The cycle does not have to be this way. It could be that in deciding to find a new way of being, we also help others around us. That would help Bob and Rita too.

For a moment, think about who — or even what — is your Bob? Bob can come in many guises. What do you embroil yourself in in order not to change yourself? Is it family dramas, other people's love lives, endless moaning and complaining about everything, saving everyone else from their pain, trying to change everyone else, a job that can't survive without you for a moment?

Many people feel self-indulgent for trying to be happy when others are suffering. But the old saying is true: by helping yourself, you do help others. Success is something we all enjoy together! And think for a moment, is happiness self-indulgent? Is inner peace something that only comes to those who are selfish? Do successful people have to be merciless? I don't believe so. I do believe, however, that being socialized to think this way is common and divisive. You may have been taught that by standing up and being the wonderful person that you are, in some way you are disrespecting those less fortunate. But other people's restrictions do not have to be yours. Learn from others with love and then listen to your inner voice.

I am not suggesting that we leave Bob to fend for himself — serving others is a gift and a total joy. However, we can complicate this process with our own internal unease. If we are experiencing greater peace within, the quality of help we are realistically able to give others will quadruple.

'I'M STICKING WITH IT, NO MATTER WHAT'

On the subject of others, so often we stay in relationships for reasons other than our own happiness. Maybe we live with the hope of our partner fulfilling a potential that we know is within them, even though we have never seen a glimmer of it being expressed. Or we feel that others will suffer if we leave, so we choose our own suffering as a way of minimal harm. Or we hold ourselves away from relationships altogether because we feel that if someone really got to know us, they wouldn't see anything good to love. Projecting a better future may give us hope, but it will only bind us into a cycle of experiencing lack in every present moment.

The situations we find ourselves in can be as complex as the beliefs we may have about them, and they will not always be easy. In life, other people may test us, challenge us and of course push every one of our buttons. Learn from these. The saying by the pioneering psychologist Carl Jung, 'Everything that irritates us about others can lead us to an understanding of ourselves' sums this up perfectly. Learn from others, as that is why they are there. Learn from them and love them. What else is there to do?

Also, let your relationships, in whatever capacity, be ones that resonate with a growing love for *yourself* as well as the other person. If you don't feel that you deserve to be treated well, or feel that another person would reject you as not worthy, then this a time to learn that loving yourself will help you to release these restrictions. If this resonates with you, then go back to those affirmations and affirm that you are lovable just as you are now and deserve to experience happiness right now in all of your relationships.

'WISHING I WAS DIFFERENT...'

Guilt and shame are some of the most punitive feelings we can have. They can lead to self-punishment, self-criticism and binding ourselves to a long-gone painful past. They will not bring peace and happiness. By feeling guilty we are saying that we have done something wrong and therefore won't allow ourselves to ever feel deserving of ease and happiness. If you do feel that you have hurt another person and are able to understand your part in this, then you will be sending love out where you may once have sent anger or hatred, betrayal or resentment. So do this and then… let it go. How does holding on to what you have done help you? How does reliving the past in your mind allow it to rest in peace?

Sometimes we may upset others even though we are only trying our best. In my life and work I have been witness to all levels of this. If you are open enough to see your part in the situation then you have travelled miles along your own journey already. Guilt is far too heavy an emotion to carry any further, so please give it up. Guilt does not create space for love.

Some of you reading this may still feel that those who have hurt *you* should be punished. Whatever you are feeling, don't be hard on yourself. Our feelings are there for a reason, so we cannot criticize ourselves for having them. Just allow yourself, from whatever viewpoint, to reach for the freedom of feeling better than you do today about this situation.

Moving back to the idea of forgiveness, are you able to forgive yourself as much as others? Remember the corridor visualization where you made the active decision to walk away from anger and towards love (see page 82). If you are carrying any guilt, shame, embarrassment or punitive feelings towards yourself or others, then please use this simple technique again. However, instead of choosing to walk in the opposite direction to anger, allow yourself to walk away from whatever it is that burdens you. You don't need to carry it any longer. Use this technique daily until you feel your guilt or burden has dissolved.

We can often feel guilty about how we treat others even when we are learning. That shows us just how hard we are on ourselves. It's time to let our feelings rest.

GIVING UP ON WHO WE THINK WE ARE

We often get to a stage in our lives where we feel that we know ourselves. We come to accept who we are, with all our little quirks, fears, reactions and ways of being. We feel these things make us who we are.

However, we are far more than the expression of our learned behaviour, experiences, mind chatter and patterns. There is a part of us that is calm and peaceful, a part that is willing to give up anger and resentment and definitely a part that is more loving and giving than we can imagine. Are you willing to give up the identity that you have created and access these other parts of yourself?

Take a moment to visualize just how happy you would be if you were at peace within. What you would be doing? Where would you be? What would you look like? In order to be that person, you will need to be willing to see that image as a possibility.

Being willing to give up who you think you are to embrace what will bring you happiness is another step forward.

'IT'S TOO MUCH TO FEEL THIS'

Diverting away from resistance also involves addressing fear. Fear can stop our progress completely. It can make us talk ourselves out of anything and also attract the situations, people and challenges that will reinforce this. When we get a buy-in from others, we have even more justification not to move forward.

Not that this will help us, of course. If we know deep down that a relationship isn't working for us, for example, but fear the pain and upheaval of making a change, that fear can keep us in a state of discomfort. Even if we are beginning to feel that we deserve the best, fear can be so strong that we won't let ourselves claim that happiness.

As Paramahamsa Yogananda taught so clearly, 'Fear throws a veil on intuition, shrouding the almighty power of your natural confidence that springs intuitively from the all-conquering soul.' When we are afraid, we can let it paralyze our ability to process, listen, learn and change.

This can lock us into despair. Despair is losing hope in what is possible. We can even feel it when we are right on the cusp of success but are so focused on what we don't have that we fail to see where we are. If we are able to bring ourselves back to a point of calm, however, we can begin to see the possibilities returning once more. Nothing is impossible with an awareness of possibilities!

A common fear on this journey of life is the loss of something before it has even arrived. How often do we fear feeling sad or experiencing failure and illness before we have even welcomed in happiness and health in the first place? We try and avoid the pain by not allowing ourselves to embrace the good. This may be because we believe the good will be fleeting or because we fear we will come to depend on it to ignite these happy feelings, so we would rather stay in pain than sample even a little happiness. In either case, the more that we allow ourselves to accept happiness, be grateful for it and stay in the feelings it brings, the less we will be focused on its potential loss.

If you find that in very happy times your mind floats away to feared situations, use your tools to bring yourself back to feeling grateful for the present moment. 'Right now I allow myself to welcome in, enjoy and be grateful for all the good in my life' resonates a lot better than 'What if something bad happens?'

If fear is coming up for you a lot, then learning to deal with it is part of your growth. Mine too. So make it the catalyst for *doing something*. Take those breaths and focus on releasing the fear rather than just sitting with it. If you can use moments of fear as a way of tapping into an inner courage, then you can learn that something different is possible. That is a real gift.

WHAT'S THE POINT?

One fear that can affect our decisions, ideas, relationships and acceptance of the joyous present throughout our whole life is the fear of our own death. This gives us an opportunity to understand the strength of our attachment to this experience of life. If we identify solely with our mind chatter or physical system as a way of understanding who or what we are, then the thought of these two systems no longer existing can bring great anxiety. However, the more we allow ourselves to delve into the learning of the great soul that we are, the more open we are to experiencing greater peace in the cycle of our own life and death and to embracing something more to come. Society as a whole does not like to talk about death and it is not good that it has become such a taboo subject for so many. But know that you are able to find an ease in your own beliefs about it and in your inner self.

Fear of death is closely tied to our strongest beliefs about life, the ones we can be very resistant to change. These may not be to our benefit. If we feel under pressure to fit everything into our allotted time, deadlines and personal milestones can become absolutely crucial. We may make the most of every moment in desperation rather than joy. Every illness may be feared as a potential life-threatening situation and the slightest signs of ageing can instigate snowballing thoughts that the end is closer than we think. If we don't find comfort in our own beliefs about death, we will live a life where every thought, action or situation has the potential to terrify us. There will be a constant fear of the future, which will bring no peace to our everyday life.

Finding comfort in our beliefs is important here. If we don't feel there is anything after the end of our physical body and this terrifies us, it would be worth affirming 'Each and every day is wonderful. I find growing comfort in the knowledge that each day of my life is filled with love and wonder.' That would feel better than fearing that each day could be a terrible end.

There are many perspectives on death. Whatever yours is, why not open up to the possibility that there could be another way of *living*? Elisabeth Kübler-Ross encapsulates this notion perfectly: 'It is not the end of the physical body that should worry us. Rather, our concern must be to live while we are alive — to release our inner selves from the spiritual death that comes with living behind a façade designed to conform to external definitions of who or what we are.'

We may not know what will happen in the rest of our life, or at the end of it, but we can embrace every step of this journey as it comes, and that will bring us the greatest peace.

EXERCISE 9: *Loving the Self*

At least once a day for the next 30 days, reinforce loving yourself in body, actions, spirit and mind.

In Body
Whenever you judge or criticize your physical body, change those patterns and see it only with love. Whenever you view a part of your body as anything below wonderful, cancel those negative thoughts and reinforce how much you love that part of your body. You can also scan through your body and mentally reinforce your love for each and every part. If a part is experiencing disease or discomfort, focus on it and send it particular love and appreciation.

In Actions
Structure one activity for yourself that's just about reinforcing your self-worth and self-love. This could range from a pampering treatment to a day with friends, a yoga class, a swim, or even booking a holiday. This is a day of pure enjoyment. No money excuses. You'll be amazed at what offers are around, what you can do for free and who will help you if you ask.

In Mind
When you find yourself resisting change in any capacity, notice your thoughts and feelings and ask yourself why they have arisen and how you could divert away from this resistance by accepting a new way of being. Give yourself permission to see what happens when you move forward in life — gently, at your own pace, being extra kind to yourself when necessary.

In Spirit
Immerse yourself in visualizing yourself in a state of total fulfilment in every area of your life. Really connect with that feeling. Visualize yourself living a life that feels fulfilled, calm, joyful and in touch with the real you. What would that new state of fulfilment be like? Enjoy feeling it.

It only takes a few moments to close your eyes and see, feel and allow yourself to embrace a new state. You will find that you are closer to it than you believe you are.

Chapter 7

Misunderstanding our Pathway to Inner Peace and Harmony:
Diverting Away from Disorder

Not to believe in the possibility of permanent peace is to disbelieve in the godliness of human nature.

— *MAHATMA GANDHI*

'Dis-order', 'dis-harmony' and 'dis-ease' describe the experience of being without order, harmony or ease. 'Dis' means 'to disconnect, reverse or lack'. How interesting that the words we use to describe suffering actually show how we suffer by not being connected to order, harmony and ease.

So far we have addressed six major misunderstandings that prevent us from embracing this connection. Now let us look at our ability to create peace and harmony within and how this is the foundation for experiencing an endless supply of peace and harmony in our inner and outer lives.

'I CAN DO THIS IN MY TIME'

It is always wonderful to look at the society that we are an incredible part of and notice its diverse aspects with gratitude. We are in an age where technology is racing forward, yet does not seem to be making our lives any easier. We appear to be involved in a growing celebrity obsession, and the emphasis is firmly on our external appearance rather than inner self.

Just because others are doing something doesn't mean that you have to do it. Why hold on to an identity that doesn't resonate with inner peace? Don't let worries about what others will think get in the way of what will bring you happiness. Do content people ever criticize you for what you are doing, or joke that you will never be as good? No, they are too busy being happy. You can be equally content if you give yourself permission.

Don't wait for someone to convince you that it is OK to learn more — just allow yourself to do it. But don't blame or criticize yourself for where you are starting from. We have already learned that we can be influenced by so many factors, and accepting yourself and where you are now is key.

So, where are you? Are you living a life where you never seem to have time to complete anything? Are there many things that you'd like to do, but you never seem to do them? Are holidays the only time when you let yourself (notice I say 'let yourself') really relax? Is your life just so busy that you have to plan time to rest rather than plan time to do things?!

We are constantly fed the message that we do not have enough time. Just look at the world around you. Here are some of the simplest examples:

- 'Lose weight for Christmas!' (If you don't do it by then you won't look your best — can you feel the time pressure and the plummeting self-worth already?)
- 'It's that time of year again where we have to decide where to go on holiday!' (Or miss out on some offers, and we don't like to feel that we will miss out, so we take on these time burdens.)
- 'It's time for you to decide what you want to do with your life.' (Or the pressure of age, income, marital status and others' expectations will land on you with great force!)
- 'Only five days to go — don't miss out!' (Miss out on what? A frantic restructuring of your next five days to fit something in you now believe you need, or you will be in a state of lack and therefore not feel good about yourself, life and what you have or own?!)

Putting a time pressure on yourself means that you have extra pressure underlying your decisions and less space just to be. How can your choices then come from a place of peace? If you are rushing through life, trying to hit your personal milestones, you only set yourself up to fail and feel bad about yourself. Give up the burden of trying so hard and watch your life be filled with joy.

I meet people whose lives are an endless whirl of activity and they don't seem to be at peace within themselves, even though they are often doing all the right things. As we've learned, this can be a form of resistance to addressing our own happiness. If we don't love ourselves enough to create the space to rest and look within in the present moment, we will stay disconnected from our inner peace.

WHY NO REST?

We cannot busy ourselves towards enlightenment or rush towards peace. The attitude that we take towards completing a task is not necessary on our inner journey —on that journey, we rest as we go. So what do you do to relax? Maybe you sit in front of the television, watch a movie, cook, call a friend, play a computer game, go to the gym or have a long hot shower. These may be pleasurable and enable you to rest and tune out of your other daily activities. However, can we really call them relaxation? They all may bring rest in one aspect, but they all involve diverting our senses and mind elsewhere. We can easily learn that this is what relaxation is — tuning out of what has been going on in the day and tuning into something else. But deep relaxation is beyond the senses and the noisy mind.

Over 15 years I have watched first myself and then others learn how to deeply relax. Only this week a student commented that she had thought she was relaxing until she started *really* relaxing. Now she can't get enough of it. Enough of what? Experiencing a part of herself that is beyond the mind chatter and so deep and peaceful that even when she has finished, her whole day is fuelled by a change in how she thinks (how she does *not* think as much) and acts. No wonder she wants more of it.

Before we look at how you can have it too, let's look at what might be happening now for you.

EVERYONE HAS IT, SO IT MUST BE NORMAL

As we mentioned in the last chapter, we appear to have accepted that stress, even continual stress, is a relatively normal state. It is true that we have an incredible capacity to perceive danger, fight, run and defend ourselves when necessary. The problems occur when we stay in this heightened state and don't fully repair, rest and rejuvenate. If we wish to regain harmony and reclaim happiness, learning how to address continual stress becomes vital.

The stress might not even be happening now. We may be living in a painful past or a dreaded future rather than the present. We may even identify ourselves according to that past. An example of this would be a person who has at one time experienced depression and now, although perfectly well, still defines themselves as having depression, even though there have been no signs of it for years.

Watch your everyday speech and listen to how you describe future events, tasks that have to be completed and potential situations. If you are feeling stressed about these, is this response making things worse?

We can become very conditioned into not believing that we can cope with situations. Then we cause ourselves twice the stress, because not only do we have to deal with the situation, but also our belief that we can't cope with it.

There is one quote by Mother Teresa that always comes to mind when I am beginning to feel any concern about my situation: 'I know God will not give me anything that I can't handle. I just wish that He didn't trust me so much.' It is a reminder that I am seeing the situation as more than what I can handle, but it's not more than I have the capacity to handle. Away from the limited mindset, everything is perfect.

At times of immense pressure, I have always reminded myself that I can cope and that any discomfort will pass. I allow myself the time to experience what I need to know in order to learn that even greater peace is possible.

There are no mistakes and no failures. You just have to keep trying new ways until you find the one that really does bring you peace and harmony. Let your mindset change from success/failure to the understanding that, for however long you are here, learning will be one step at a time.

I would love to see a world where we don't see 'failure' as such a full stop and an opportunity to feel bad about ourselves. It really is just another step along the perfect journey of knowing and changing. If we are moving towards happiness, every time we aren't happy, what a great point of learning that is! We can even say, 'And now I choose to feel something different.' Never forget that we are able to choose a good feeling and experience.

SWAPPING LIKE FOR LIKE

Along this path of change, we may, however, relieve the stress in one part of our life and move on without actually addressing the real issue. For example, we leave a job that doesn't resonate with what we really want to be doing, but take with us the mindset that the workload is unmanageable, we aren't sure we can cope and this had better be the right job as we don't want to experience the upheaval of moving again. Guess what is likely to happen in our next job? Relationships, too, can hold the same themes. We can move away from a relationship that doesn't reinforce how wonderful we are and into a new one. However, if our mind is still on our past one and we are still feeling we aren't good enough, the new relationship may well end up the same.

The process of change is about allowing a new state to arise, not just swapping one thing for another without swapping how we really feel about it. And this new state involves being in touch with the peace and harmony within.

Students often ask what they need to do to access this. You don't need to do anything in particular to begin with, except allow yourself to move away from what binds you to not feeling good enough. If you can take the time to really invest in appreciating, accepting, caring for and loving yourself, then you will notice how situations will change, but most of all your *reactions* towards them will change. This opens the door to allowing peace into your heart.

ORGANIZATION

It is very helpful to understand how organization can help us when we are diverting away from disorder. If you find that your life currently looks totally disorganized, does this resonate with the calm and peace that you are hoping for?

Have a look at your home and office. Are you constantly running around trying to find things in a random unorganized mess? If so, then your life is already more complicated than it need be. What changes could make your environment a place of peace and tranquillity?

You don't have to have a complete life overhaul. Just take note of when you get frustrated by your home environment, your messy office or even the state of your car boot. Where does the chaos in your life cause even more disorder for you?

Being open to organizing your life so that you have more time for yourself and more time to rest. Organize your time so that you can take a lunch break every single day. Build in activities that resonate with feeling healthy, nourished and happy.

PUSHING IT DOWN

Over the past decade, I have worked with more and more clients suffering from a variety of anxiety and panic attacks. I know how scary these can feel. Often the clients will see them as the problem. However, to me these are just the symptoms of an internal unease.

We can address the build-up of anxiety with relative ease using proper breathing and relaxation techniques. Treating the cause of the problem, however, involves addressing not only why the panic is occurring but the patterns and beliefs that are holding the person in this state of unease. Both approaches are important.

Think of a Jack-in-the-box. At times we can push down our unease and get on with life, but it may take only one small incident to flick the latch and out it pops, engulfing us in anxiety, panic and despair.

The physical reactions can often terrify clients as much as the emotions. But they can cease completely when we address the underlying unease and let rest and relaxation flow through us.

There are certain underlying trends that come to light here, all related to the lack of connection to our real self. Extreme panic and anxiety often occur:

- when we try to hide our true self from others in case they see we really aren't a good or worthy person
- when we try to please others and disregard our own wishes
- when we live with deep self-loathing
- when we always have to do more and more to prove our worth
- when we have to pretend to be far more than we feel we are and can never let our vulnerabilities be seen
- when we feel restricted or bound to a life that does not resonate with any personal fulfilment, purpose or expression.

In all these situations, we are carrying such a heavy burden that it's no wonder there is some form of reaction.

Acknowledging that we have nothing to prove is key to moving forward here. We have nothing to hide from anyone; no one will judge us as harshly as we have ourselves. Loving ourselves more every day and allowing others to see the real us is a process of gentle change that will lead to peace. And now is the day to start.

MINDLESSNESS

We are ever-present to the mind because even when we are not actively tuning into our thoughts and observing them, we can still be experiencing life under their influence. But there is more to tap into — the divinity that flows through each and every one of us.

Getting in touch with this divine self is about taking an inward journey. As Swami Muktananda states:

The Sages who saw the Self
said many things about the Self.
But only if you meditate and go within
can you experience it fully.

So I would like you to consider three new stages to your journey: relaxation, concentration and meditation. These will all help you to quieten the busy mind noise and tune into an inner element of yourself that you may not have experienced. I'll give you a simple relaxation technique here that was taught to me by my teacher Ernest Coates and a meditation technique later in this chapter. You don't have to go to a lot of trouble to do either of these — having a particular room, the right incense burning or a specially-designed cushion to sit on, for example. You need nothing more than yourself, your inner permission and a small amount of room in a quiet, warm, undisturbed space.

As to what time of day will bring you the greatest benefits, you can use your relaxation technique at any time, as a prelude to calming yourself before sleep or even in bed to help you fall asleep each night.

As for meditation, first thing in the morning will have a profound impact on your day. Why not wake up 20 minutes early? Or, if you find that it is impossible for you to have space in the morning, you could rearrange a part of your day to create 20 minutes. This could be in your office at lunchtime or before work, or even in the park, if that is your only space. I used to get into work early to meditate and start my day in touch. Now I find that my mornings at home work best. Wherever you are, it is surprising how a few moments can change your whole day, your whole life.

RELAXATION AT LAST

Deep relaxation involves directing your attention away from outer sensory input and fully focusing on initiating relaxation and calm in every part of your being.

If you find that you have a great many things on your mind, jot them down on a piece of paper so that you can free yourself up to rest and relax. Why carry what you don't need?

If possible, lie down on your back with a cover over you to keep you warm and adjust your clothing so that you are comfortable. Let your eyes close. Allow your arms to rest a little way from the sides of your body, so that they don't interfere with it. Let the backs of your hands rest on the floor so that the palms are face upwards. Let your legs gently rest apart with the feet and ankles relaxing out to the sides. If you are unable to lie on your back or are pregnant, please seek help to find a position that supports you on your side instead.

The breath is key when calming the mind and body. It is the link between the two. Full, deep and slow breathing, filling and emptying all areas of the lungs, is important. A few deep breaths can instantly calm the mind and body. You can visualize breathing out any stress or tension from your physical or emotional system. This is a great way to begin any practice of relaxation.

To relax body and mind together, we begin by focusing and holding our full awareness on each part of the body. Then we visualize each part relaxing, feel each part relaxing and, if there is any pain, tension or stress in the body, visualize this dispersing.

Do not rush the practice — take time to acknowledge each part of the body and allow it to fully relax before moving on.

Work through the body in the following order:

- Focus on the toes. Relax the toes.
- Focus on the feet. Relax the feet.
- Focus on the lower legs. Relax the lower legs.
- Focus on the upper legs. Relax the upper legs.
- Focus on the buttocks. Relax the buttocks.
- Focus on the back. Relax the back.
- Focus on the pelvic area. Relax the pelvic area.
- Focus on the abdomen. Relax the abdomen.
- Focus on the chest. Relax the chest.
- Focus on the fingers. Relax the fingers.
- Focus on the hands. Relax the hands.
- Focus on the lower arms. Relax the lower arms.
- Focus on the upper arms. Relax the upper arms.
- Focus on the shoulders. Relax the shoulders.
- Focus on the neck and throat. Relax the neck and throat.
- Focus on the mouth and chin. Relax the mouth and chin.
- Focus on the nose and cheeks. Relax the nose and cheeks.
- Focus on the eyes. Relax the eyes.
- Focus on the ears. Relax the ears.
- Focus on the back of the head. Relax the back of the head.
- Focus on the top of the head. Relax the top of the head.
- Focus on the forehead. Relax the forehead.

These are the 22 sensitive parts of the body that can induce full relaxation when focused upon and consciously relaxed. You can repeat this sequence two or three more times.

If thoughts pop up, acknowledge them and then let them go by and move your awareness back to the practice. They have come up for a reason and you can see their presence as a gift before you once again detach yourself from them.

If emotions rise up, that is also OK. Once again, don't feel that you have to block anything. Just allow this process to be for your highest good.

If you find that at any point you feel uncomfortable, just move back to the awareness of your breathing and the notion of calm within each breath that you take.

To induce an even deeper relaxation, work in the reverse order, from the head down to the toes. Try both and experience the vast difference between them.

You may find that to begin with you are practising for five to ten minutes and you gradually increase this. As with all of your process of change, work with what is comfortable for you. There is a great joy in letting go of conditioned time pressures and enjoying real connection and relaxation.

You may find as you progress that you use this technique prior to a meditation. I use it regularly, both as a prelude to further practices and on its own to induce a state of rest, and benefit from it immensely.

NOW CONCENTRATE...

Concentration is an important stage on our pathway to peace. We may have experienced what it feels like to concentrate on a painful memory or emotion, but may not have directed our awareness to peace and calm or used it to tap into the deeper elements of ourselves.

Bring to mind a time when you had to focus on what someone was trying to tell you and block out distractions to hear what they were saying. You had to focus your awareness and absorb yourself into it. You're now going to use this same skill in meditation to experience the peace within. You are going to learn how to direct your attention to a point of calm and peace.

Meditation is practised by many traditions around the world. You may discover many different meditation practices as you go through life. Enjoy this discovery and remember there is no right way, only what is right for you.

The word 'meditation' comes from the Latin *meditari*, 'to heal'. If you were to ask me *what* we are healing, I would say that apart from rejuvenating and calming our whole self, we are healing the disconnection with our real self — the authentic part of us that is in touch with the whole universe. The learning comes through our experience of it rather than reading about it or scientifically analyzing it.

To begin with, find a space in which to sit. You don't have to be in the lotus position or any rigid, stereotypical pose if this isn't possible. You can even sit on a chair if you are unable to sit comfortably cross-legged, with or without the aid of cushions underneath your bottom or behind your back to encourage an upright and lengthened spine. I have sat and meditated in my car with great ease. If you are unable to sit at all and can only lie down, then please just be as comfortable as you can. Do not place any restrictions on the external when the whole point is to go within. However, a quiet space, undisturbed time, a blanket around your shoulders to keep you warm and your phone turned off will be a good start.

When you have adjusted your clothes and position and prevented any disturbances, you can allow your eyes to close. Check that your posture is comfortable and body is warm enough. You may feel, to begin with, that a few rounds of scanning though your body in the relaxation mentioned above will help you to focus within.

Watching the breath is a wonderful way to begin meditation. Just acknowledging your breathing brings you back to the gift that it really is — the exchange of energy, in and out.

Find your awareness of the breath in the way that feels most comfortable to you. Some people like to hold their awareness at the tip of the nose and observe the breath as it flows in and out from this point — the cool breath that slowly flows in and the slightly warmer air that flows out. Others prefer to follow the whole journey of the breath as it flows in through the nostrils, down the throat, into the lungs and then back up and out of the body once again. Or you may prefer to watch the rise and fall of the abdomen as the body breathes. You don't have to become attached to this process. It is as if your body is breathing and you are the observer.

As you develop, you may begin to notice that there is a great peace in the pause between the inhalation and exhalation, a great rest and calm where you are in touch and connected. You may notice that your inhalation and exhalation are different lengths. As you relax, you will find that they become more even. Notice that you do not force, strain or jerk your breath in and out — you allow it to move.

As you turn your awareness towards your breathing, notice how you allow yourself the gift of being fully present, connected, yet equally in a new state that you may never have experienced before. Persevere with kindness and dedication.

As with your relaxation, you can begin with allowing yourself ten minutes then work up to 20 minutes daily as you feel ready. This state of calm and peace will become the foundation for your whole day. Later, you can add many other techniques to your meditation. However, take the time to find what is right for you and be patient with yourself. There's no need to rush.

Through meditation we can reach a point where we can see the world with broader vision. We go beyond just the appearances of life and begin to process the reality of it. We are no longer attached to the constant processing of stimuli and can begin to experience another dimension of our real self.

When I was delving deeper into my learning and asked a swami what should I do next (notice I thought I still had to do something), the response was: 'Learn to love your meditation.' That was the greatest advice.

Chapter 8

Misunderstanding our Personal Fulfilment: Diverting Away from Dissatisfaction

Here is a test to find whether your mission on earth is finished:
If you're alive,
It isn't.

—*RICHARD BACH*

We really only need to address a few questions in life to understand our personal journey. Although these questions may sound simple, like 'What am I here to experience?', they often instigate great debate. The debate is not just about figuring out the answer, but about allowing ourselves to make that answer a reality in this lifetime.

So often I hear people talk about what they want to do in their outer life, only to follow up with reasons why that cannot or should not happen. So far, we have addressed seven misunderstandings which may play a part in this. The overall misunderstanding is about how *possible* we feel total fulfilment is for us. Do you believe that your affirmations will work, that you will reap their rewards and that you are as capable of being happy, healthy and fulfilled as other people?

As children, we are constantly asked what we want to be when we grow up. It is as if in infancy, possibilities seem real, both to the child and the adult questioning them. Have you ever heard a five-year-old say they want to be an astronaut and go to the moon and then give ten minutes of careful reasoning why NASA may not accept them on the basis of not being clever enough or fit enough and why it's unlikely to happen anyway, as only a few people ever get to go and, knowing their luck, it won't be them? Of course not. As adults we often feel we know better. Better by limiting our own lives? My question to you is, what is this restriction that kicks in and what does it feel like for you?

Let's move forward to our school-leaving years. Once again we are asked what we would like to do with our life. Now there is a difference. We have formed opinions of our skills, talents and possibilities. We have developed greater patterns and levels of self-worth and we have a greater view of the external world, although a somewhat restricted one, due to lack of experience. We may not know what we want to do, but we are very aware that this is a time when we are expected to choose. And if we don't know, it is amazing how we can be directed towards something in which we have no true interest.

This brings about two major issues about misunderstanding our personal fulfilment. First, the influence of expectation, conformity and failure. Second, the influence of logic and reason in the decision-making process, rather than feeling.

I remember clearly having a careers interview, aged 15, which lasted no more than 20 minutes and didn't involve me having any real input. I was told that journalism or something similar would be great for me, as I was a people person. Now I hated English literature, was dyslexic and didn't enjoy reading. Very appropriate. Not the career officer's fault of course — he was only trying to help. The point is, my own inner joy of expression was not addressed and this was an older person telling me what was appropriate for me based on very little information.

Let's look at the information available to you now. Think about the gifts and skills you have. Do you have a talent for organizing and planning? Are you drawn to music, art, singing, numbers, sport? Have you ever pushed your passions into a hobby rather than built them into your whole life?

We can make very fixed personal agreements with ourselves at very young ages. We tell ourselves that we know what we are going to be and what will make us happy. Then, as we live out our life, we may feel that we have failed to put some of these ideas into practice. Take a look at a younger you — what did you want your life to be like? What dreams haven't you fulfilled yet? Of course some of these may no longer be relevant, but surely you wanted to be really happy? Are you really happy now?

You may think that the die has already been cast and you have to live with your choices. But choices are for every stage of life. You only need to change your current ones to change the direction of your future. There is no right age to discover what you want to do with your life. You only have the present moment, and that's all that you need.

If you feel that change isn't possible, you may be making some of the following assumptions:

- *'A change seems so risky at this stage of my life.'* Considering that we are not aware of the length of our life, how can we presume that we are at any stage of it? Why make the assumption that you are too old to be happy or too old to retrain, or even too old to try something new? This will only bind you to dissatisfaction.

- *'A change would mean a loss of income.'* A loss of income may result, possibly temporarily; however, is that more important than the loss of your fulfilment? Also, know that you are able to create a life of abundance. It is amazing how you can find new ways to deal with things if you are acting according to your inner sense of purpose.

- *'A change would mean that I'd have to retrain with people a lot younger than me.'* Yes — younger people, not ravenous wolves. And you have the gift of experience and haven't lost the ability to learn (though you may have lost your *belief* in that ability). No one, whatever their age, is better or worse than you.

- *'I'm too old.'* Once again, in the great scheme of life you may have anything between 1 and 100 (approximately of course) years ahead of you. What is old?

- *'I couldn't fit it in.'* We're back to being time resistant again. Restructuring, reorganizing and creating the space for peace will help you to fit in whatever you want.

- *'I can't take in information like I used to as a child.'* That's great, because your new life does not warrant the approach of a child, it warrants you being you right now, so you are 100 per cent perfect.

- *'I want a rest at this time of life.'* Does that mean 'rest to relax' or 'rest in a state of happiness and fulfilment'? You can do both — you can build relaxation into your life, finding greater peace, *and* find the outer fulfilment that brings you great joy.

- *'There are no opportunities for people my age.'* Be aware of the reality that will show up to match the thought energy that you are sending out. On the other hand, it's amazing what can show up in your life when you are willing to see it as a possibility.

- *'What if I don't like it?'* We may be scared to try something new in case we disappoint ourselves or others. But remember there is no failure, just one more step along the path of life.

- *'Maybe I'm just thinking I can have it all.'* It depends what your definition of 'all' is and (back to our attachments) why 'all' matters so much to you. However, in terms of fulfilling your dreams, you have the ability to experience any part of life that you choose to in one way or another.

Making any change at all may sound like a drastic move, but living a rewarding life doesn't mean running away from our current situation, but using it as a springboard to something even more fulfilling. If we let go of what isn't serving us and initiate simple changes in ourselves, these changes can vibrate through our whole life.

NEW PERSPECTIVES ON OLD SITUATIONS

At certain times we may accept that the way things are is the way they will stay. But we don't know what is around the corner, so it's not worth giving up before we've walked around to see. If the here and now isn't really where we want to be, we can take a new perspective and visualize it looking a little different. The future will follow in that same positive outlook.

We may be feeling despondent because we have viewed our disappointments as failures that are a reflection on us personally. But now we can begin to understand that they have simply been stages of growth on the way to what is best for us.

When change comes into our life, in whatever form, let's see if we can flow with it instead of resisting it. Situations may arise that will test us or challenge us, but when they do, we can simply look at our reaction to them and ask ourselves, 'Does this help me to see the truth in this situation? Does this help me to find happiness and peace?' Letting go of our usual (and possibly restricted) way of being will free us up so much.

WAKING UP

Waking up to new ideas is opening up to living at a new level of consciousness. If we can lose the stereotypes we are often fed, we will see that so much more is on offer. In fact, we are already waking up to new possibilities just by being open to them existing.

Which ones we take is entirely up to us, of course. There is no right way on this journey — we all have our own individual ways of experiencing fulfilment and happiness. We can use regrets to bind us to our past and find reasons why we should be bound to unhappiness, as we have seen, but the present moment is always ours to embrace. If we can release our anger, resentment and guilt, then slowly we can allow ourselves to reclaim happiness.

We all have the ability to choose a different present and, consequently, a very different future. Never forget this.

Also, don't sacrifice your happiness to make others feel better. Not rocking the boat is a very common reason for people not embracing what feels right for them.

But this will only lead to inner unrest and this will be always expressed in some way — frustration doesn't just disappear. Remember that you can't change other people, but you can start changing yourself and working *with* other people to move towards happiness. And the more you find happiness within, the more love you will have to give.

TAPPING INTO THE EXPRESSION OF THE REAL SELF

When I was younger, I desperately wanted to feel different, but I didn't understand this fully, so I held on to the belief that I had to be somewhere different, look different and act differently in order to show the world who I was. Ironically, the only place where I *wasn't* different was inside. So as I walked along my pathway of life I found moments of success were followed by immense dissatisfaction again. It is those moments of disconnection and struggle that I am asking you to consider now, and how we can reclaim our connection to our real self.

It can be difficult to understand ourselves on a deeper level if our thoughts are racing around with endless chatter, criticisms, judgements and fantasies. Sometimes the mind feels so busy and loud, even out of control, that we feel it is our entire existence. We need to make space to let our inner voice come through.

Imagine you are at a busy party. Your intuitive feelings are there, sitting in one corner of the room. They are speaking away, providing you with valuable insights, but you are at the other end of the room and totally focused on what you are doing, so you don't hear them, see them or even recognize that they could be relevant to you. When someone does point this out, with all the chatter going on at this party you accept that you are never going to hear them anyway, so carry on with what you are doing. Maybe you did once make the effort to walk over and ask them what they were trying to tell you, and it wasn't what you wanted to hear, so you haven't bothered to repeat the process. Either consciously or unconsciously, you are staying with the noisy chatter of the party rather than having that one valuable conversation with your real self.

There are many reasons why we don't want to listen to our own inner knowing, but even when we are ignoring it, it is affecting us. The reason why we are feeling that inner unease is that we aren't allowing ourselves to hear what is really best for us.

When clients feel totally confused about a decision, I ask them to close their eyes, take four deep breaths and with each out-breath just sink into the chair. After that I ask them the question they are pondering and ask them for their very first response to it. They clear the chatter of their mind and the answer pops out clear as anything. Sometimes they hesitate, as they learn how to distinguish between what they want the answer to be and what it really is, or even try to quickly tap into logic and reason, so we just have a few more breaths and repeat the process and then the answer comes out.

Then they may become upset as the reality of their situation becomes clear to them. Often they immediately explain why they cannot, should not, will not accept that this answer is right for them. Some will say that I forced it out of them. I will be silent, facing away from them, providing space for them to tap into their feelings.

Listening to your inner knowing may feel strange to you at first, as you may feel unsure whether you can trust it. Start gently by asking yourself what feels right for you and your life. Your own inner guidance will enable you to make the choices that are right for your highest good.

I am not asking you to forsake a balanced approach. Use all of the gifts that are available to you. If you are able to use your gifts of organization, for example, to make your dreams come true, then do so. Allow your inner feeling and thinking sides to work together to create the life that you want to be living. Becoming aware of not over-indulging your thinking in your decisions is key. Allowing through your own inner feelings will support your inner fulfilment and joy rather than just the fulfilment of your egoic mind and satisfaction.

Of course other people can easily reinforce why it is best for us to stay stuck and unfulfilled. They are possibly doing the same. Remember that they may not feel comfortable with the new state that we are embracing. That's OK — we can only be where we wish to be and let others do the same. Try not to let others' opinions be more powerful than your own feelings.

At times of difficulty the question is, 'Where do I turn for help?' The answer is simple: calm yourself, breathe, go within and then ask yourself whom it's best to talk to. If no one feels currently available, then don't worry, as you know, through all of the work we've been doing together, how to be open to attracting help from people who will nurture your inner wishes rather than squash them. We may feel that the people close to us should be able to offer us all the help we need. But be open to welcoming in new people who can offer new perspectives and insights.

When I met my husband, within four days we were already talking about getting married, and within two months of spending time together we were married. That was eight years ago and we are happier and more fulfilled by our connection every day. In case you are dismissing us as hopeless romantics searching desperately for love, I have to say I wasn't consciously looking when we met. My logical, analytical self, along with everyone I knew, could have written an encyclopaedia full of reasons not to marry this person I barely knew, but my inner feelings knew it was right.

Your own life will bring you situations that are right for you if you listen to your inner self and are open to acting upon your truth.

If you are having difficulty tapping into what you are feeling and are relying very heavily on your thinking, there are some simple yet effective ways to ignite this new connection within yourself.

First, take a look at the simple decisions you take every day: what to eat, what to do on your day off, what to read, and so on. Pause and consider what feels right for you. Set aside what you *usually* do or feel you *should* do. If you think you ought to eat a salad because it will be healthy but you feel like eating soup, or think you should go out and socialize at the weekend when you really feel like having a hot bath and watching a movie, look at what will make you *feel good*. That is the gauge of whether a decision is right for you.

To take this one step further, if you feel at a loss as there are too many choices available, go back to those breaths, enjoy those moments of calm, and now write down five pleasurable activities that will help you to feel good. Choose which resonates total peace within you. Start with smaller decisions and slowly, as you get more comfortable with feeling your way to a more peaceful state, you can move along the path towards your new life decisions.

Some questions to ponder (please note in answering these that it is your *feelings* that are important):

- What activities do you love doing?
- What would bring you great feelings of joy?
- Would you be willing to act upon your feelings to find greater fulfil-ment in your career, relationships and lifestyle?

Remember that you deserve to find fulfilment in every aspect of your life.

WATCHING, LEARNING AND CREATING SPACE

Life can bring us situations that involve trying to figure out how to move forward in the easiest and quickest way. Finding clarity at such times allows us to under-stand when we are flowing with the possible and when we are resisting it.

Certain situations can sweep us up and swirl us around in a whirlwind until we feel we have fallen to the ground. These may be emotional situations and I am not suggesting that you hide your emotions, as they are there to be experienced. How-ever, see whether you could take a moment to draw back so that you can see the situation more clearly. If you realize you are being carried away by negative thoughts, bring your awareness back to your breath and ask yourself, 'Is this bringing me peace? Am I willing to let go of this?'

When you are creating the space to see the truth of a situation, the answers can show up when you least expect them. When I started writing this book I borrowed a laptop and went to a local café. That didn't work for me because I was constantly hungry and distracted. But in the two visits before I realized that I was best away from fresh quiches, watching people and talking to the staff, I had some insightful experiences.

One morning I had been questioning whether I should give up seeing clients one to one and make a permanent shift towards workshops, talks and seminars. Then I sat back with my delicious lunch and watched an event unfold before me like beautiful poetry.

A father had brought his teenage son to the café to speak to him about his behaviour. He was fraught with worry about the boy's drug-taking and general lack of lust for life. The son was horrified that his father knew about the drugs. I watched the most heated and emotional exchange, which ended up with the son walking out and the father being left in the café very upset. I carried on with my lunch … until the father asked me what he should do. There was no way I could have avoided hearing every detail of the exchange, even with industrial ear-plugs, so I guess he figured I knew all about it. We spoke, then he went home.

Before he left, though, he asked me what I was doing. I told him that I was a psychologist and was writing a book, although not really focusing on it. As he left, he said, 'Don't give it up — you're obviously meant to be doing it.'

That is called divine timing.

Enjoy similar moments showing up in your life. Enjoy watching how your life gets easier as you move away from the struggle within yourself. Enjoy simply asking for a change and watching that change show up. At first you may notice small, subtle alterations in your life and everything appearing to flow with ease. You may find that other people start to notice a difference in you. You may even find that situations that you have always hoped for turn up. Most importantly, you will notice how you feel as a new state of being evolves. Welcome them all into your life with gratitude … and *reclaim your own deep joy and happiness.*

EXERCISE 10: *Three-Part Action Plan*

Part 1

Now is the time to create your pathway to that fulfilled life.

Go back to the first exercise (page 30) and once again write down, from where you are now, your ideas, hopes and wishes for your new self and life.

Now go back to the third exercise (page 41) and create a new set of affirmations which will support you in moving towards this reality. Remember to phrase these positively, in the present tense, and to lay claim to them with your heart as well as your mind, as emotional investment is key. Include any diversions that you feel will support you, for example.

DIVERSION 1: 'I see myself as a loving, divine and blessed being. I love myself just as I am.'

DIVERSION 2: 'I choose to let my life flow with love, peace and fulfilment. I am strong and powerful and know what is right for me.'

DIVERSION 3: 'I allow my inner happiness to flourish without the need to rely on feeling attached and restricted. Fulfilment flows through me always.'

DIVERSION 4: 'I allow myself to feel safe, secure and provided for now and always. I have confidence in my ability to create a life that resonates with plenty and stability.'

DIVERSION 5: 'Releasing my anger, guilt, resentment and pain makes me feel light, peaceful and free. I allow love to flow into me.'

DIVERSION 6: 'I love every part of myself in mind, body and spirit. I find the wonder in being myself and embrace myself fully.'

DIVERSION 7: 'Peace and harmony flow through me always. I give myself time to relax.'

DIVERSION 8: 'I love listening to my intuition, trusting that it is my truth and for my highest good. I allow myself to reclaim a fulfilled life.'

Part 2

Now for action! Don't worry — this isn't a 300-item 'to do' list! Just write down five steps you can take to begin to create a life that resonates with your joy and fulfilment. Examples could be starting a hobby, organizing a relaxing weekend, applying for a new educational course or making an effort to see your friends. Go with where your feelings take you. And remember that you deserve it.

Part 3

Listen to your state of being right now and let peace and happiness flow through you. Give yourself the time and space to experience the deeper elements of yourself. This will keep your connection to your real self alive. Address any resistance to not relaxing, resting and meditating in a short daily practice. Persevere, learn and allow yourself to enjoy the beginnings of a new you.

In Conclusion

The essence of faith is to believe that the unseen is as real as the seen.

—*PARAMAHAMSA HARIHARANANDA*

This journey that we have taken together has involved addressing many different misunderstandings which can arise and how we can divert away from their unfortunate consequences and towards our birthright of peace, harmony and happiness.

You may notice that right now you feel fired up with drive and determination. Hold that feeling, for you have created it and can tap into it anytime you wish.

We can, however, sometimes find that old patterns creep in or that we are faced with new situations where we are not sure what to do. Learning doesn't just happen by reading a book and absorbing knowledge, but by being out in the world and putting that knowledge into practice. So allow your new understandings to filter into your whole life, and if you face challenges or new situations, know that not only are you able to cope, but what lies before you is an opportunity to change.

If at any time you feel discomfort within, use this book as a gentle reminder of what you can do to change this feeling to one of ease and peace. Each time you look at a chapter (or even the whole book) again, you will notice how the layers of the onion gradually start to peel away.

You may have been wearing your 'I can't see any help' glasses for far too long, so they are worth changing too. If you are open to receiving help, it can shine through to you. Don't prescribe how it will arrive, just allow yourself to move away from your pain.

We can picture the pattern of learning as a spiral: sometimes challenges we have had before come round again but in a slightly different form. Sometimes we feel that we have dealt with these issues already, so why are they here again? However, this time around we may be able to understand why they are showing up in our life. And more importantly we can begin to create a different experience which does not resonate with the disharmony that originally attracted these situations to us.

FAQS

As we move through this process of learning, questions often come up. Here are a few of the most common:

How will others react to me when I choose to make positive changes to my life?

We don't know exactly how others will react when we make changes, although we may have a few ideas, and we have two choices here: we can either focus with dread on possible confrontations and disappointments — which will only help create even more fearful situations — or we can use the creative power of our own intention to direct our energy towards peaceful situations for our highest good.

Remember that by changing, we may rattle those who are still holding on to their well-oiled restricted beliefs and suffering. That is *their* choice. We cannot live our life according to *their* beliefs and expect *our* happiness to arrive.

The ironic part is that if we don't choose to leave behind our limiting ways of being, we don't give these relevant others permission to do the same. 'Anything for a quiet life' or even 'I don't want to rock the boat' won't be just at our expense, it will be at theirs too. We may feel that we are protecting others by not changing, but we are really just keeping those others fenced in, exactly where they are now.

Countless times people ask me for help in finding peace in a relationship. However, if they don't choose to find peace within themselves, then how can they possibly ask that of others? If we allow ourselves to find peace within and live a life that resonates with happiness, then we will be doing all we can for other people too. We will also be opening up a new self to be embraced in a new way. You may be surprised how your relationships change when you actually let them.

Of course the people around you may change or they may not — you don't know and neither do I. You can only create a nurturing environment for your own growth and allow others to see what you are doing. So, let others be who they are right now and focus your attention on your own unlimited possibilities.

Here's something that may help: at the first chance that you get, stand by a puddle, a pond or even a sink full of water. See how still the water can be. Now drop something very small into the centre of it and watch the tiny ripples affect the whole body of water. They will reach out to the edge and then ripple back into the centre and leaves or other debris on the surface may bob up and down. This shows what happens when the power of your thoughts reaches out and comes back and affects your life in every way.

Now, when the water has settled again, drop two small particles (leaves, drops of water, twigs, etc.) into two different parts of the water at the same time. See how they both create ripples and these actually cross over and form a beautiful pattern — a delightful new interaction. Now the whole body of water is affected by these two different waves. That is exactly what happens in the universe. Our lives affect others and create greater ripples and patterns which reach out and create our experiences.

If you are ever concerned about others or even frustrated by their reactions, remember that everything that you do will be sending out a ripple into their lives. Let them choose what they do with that new vibration. You don't need to do any more than send out your own love and peace for others to be affected in a positive way.

How do I cope in new and positive ways?

As you go through the process of change, your reactions to situations and challenges will evolve too. So don't be hard on yourself if initially you find new reactions are uncomfortable. If you need to cry, let yourself cry. If you need to work through the anger of disappointment or betrayal, allow yourself to do so. Know that the more you invest in your own truth, the more you will naturally regain a sense of harmony and inner ease.

Whatever life brings, remind yourself that even though you may sometimes need to give yourself time to heal, you can put on your 'able to cope' glasses. Keep that connection with your breathing and ensure you have time to rest and go within and touch that stillness and peace. These times will provide you with the nurturing and connection that you are really seeking; the deep inner reassurance that you are going to be OK.

What if I actually succeed?

Like putting on a pair of new shoes, something slightly different can feel strange for the first few steps. You may be surprised to see small successes coming your way and not know how to react. Don't be concerned — in those moments you've seen what is possible. What a wonderful acknowledgement for you. Now make the choice to be grateful for your success and welcome in even more by saying, '*Thank you.*' It is that simple.

If you notice doubt creeping in, or your usual 'Well, that's just a coincidence, it doesn't usually come so easily' mindset returning, allow yourself to shift towards 'I have seen what is possible and experienced it as my truth.' After all, there's no point in a new truth turning up only for you to send it away again.

When life does get easier, notice whether you feel any resistance to the space that opens up for you. Don't busy yourself up as drama and stress leave your life. Create something wonderful in their place.

If you find yourself fearing the loss of your success, then once again move back to the acknowledgement that in the great scheme of your journey you are always safe, supported, loved and provided for. Don't talk yourself out of succeeding by fearing failure in the future that hasn't happened yet. Let a glimpse of success be seen as confirmation that you are on the right path rather than a cause for fear.

If you don't truly believe that happiness can appear in your life, or maybe that joy can't come without pain, allow yourself to see your life as a pathway where pain doesn't have to be inevitable.

Use your emotions as your gauge. When you are naturally happy, at peace, calm and joyful, then you are in touch with what is right for you and success will follow.

What if the next step is too scary?

Every step that you take on this journey will be at your own pace, so there is no rush. Your emotions will tell you when you are trying to move on too quickly. Don't push yourself or burden yourself with 101 things you must achieve. Where's the peace in that? Rather, come up with just two or three new actions you could take to bring yourself closer to happiness.

Each time that you become aware of the possibility of doing things differently, or even of a particular way that you have been acting, view this as a true gift. It is the key to opening the door to new experiences. Why not pat yourself on the back and enjoy the present instead of feeling worried about the next step? If you can say 'Well done!' for seeing the truth of your situation, you can move forward with even more self-love and kindness, and we can't have enough of that!

What if I find myself reverting back to old patterns?

Again, this is a part of your incredible learning journey, so don't be hard on yourself. It will show you even more clearly that a different way is possible. Maybe you had to revert for a while before you could really believe that.

If you find yourself reverting to old patterns, simply move back, with love and kindness, to the first misunderstanding of your true divine nature and allow yourself to reconnect with the idea that there is already a part of you that is complete and magnificent. You are not going back to the beginning here, you are just absorbing the information at a deeper level with greater insight and understanding, and that is the beauty of real growth.

What if the people who are in my life now don't fully resonate with my desire for happiness and peace?

Remember those ripples in the puddle. If we are sending out a desire for love, peace and fulfilment and someone in our life reinforces anger and pain, then we will notice this even more. Remember that we are not here to judge another's journey, just learn about our own.

You can use your emotions to know what is right for you in your life right now and what is not. Be open to discovering how you feel. Breathe, relax and allow yourself to hear your truth. So often, people are confused by the clutter of thoughts, analysis, logic and emotions all jumbled together within them. Allow yourself to find that calm space within.

As far as acting upon your inner feelings, they are coming from you and no one else, so how can they be wrong for you? They are telling you that something even more incredible is possible for you.

Allow yourself to embrace situations that resonate with your total happiness. You deserve this. We all do.

How can I learn to deal with the awkward people who are in my life?

By being open to seeing the truth without self-criticism. It is very easy to see someone else's behaviour as an annoyance, but if you are able to see that maybe you are also behaving this way and resonating in the same suffering (I know we don't like to see this, but it's true), or have the same need as the person who is agitating you, even if it's expressed in a different way, you can address this.

This is the beauty of relationships: you look at how you are in them, allow yourself to see the truth of the situation and then have the opportunity to address why it is affecting you so much.

Remember that you don't need to hold onto other people's way of being. You don't need to prove how different you are from them either. Just learn how to be fully at peace within yourself and you will begin to see the same divine spark in everyone and everything.

PUTTING IT ALL TOGETHER

You were born perfect, although maybe you don't see it now. You were as incredible then as you are now. In fact there has never been any stage where you have not been a divine being, one incredible part of humanity…

Now is the time to reconnect with the rest. Separation doesn't bring peace. Remember how we began by discussing the small connections that we can make with others? A small acknowledgement of connection will help you to feel part of this wonderful universe, not a stranger to it.

Countless times, clients will comment how people they look up to have such perfect lives. They feel so separate from them — and from people who are teaching them to be happy. Take a moment to think about how separate you feel from me. You may have found a whole multitude of reasons for this. But the same divine spark of magnificence is within us all. Acknowledging that will bring you closer to peace and happiness. There are no divides, only an opportunity to embrace.

As you take this journey and begin to invest in your daily relaxation, you will begin to experience feelings of peace and ease that you never dreamed were possible. Persevere with kindness and give yourself the time to learn more day by day.

As you move on to begin a daily meditation practice and absorb yourself in the stillness within, you will find that you tap into a divine self that is beyond your thoughts, beyond your attachment as only being your physical body, and beyond your struggles. For these are not you. As you allow yourself to experience this real self, you will realize that there is no need to strive for outer fulfilment, as you already have everything you need within you.

You can now journey within, where learning and growth are infinite, and the reward will be your true state of connection and happiness. The outer journey of your life can then flow with joy rather than be a struggle for survival.

I have always known that I would write books, although if you had told me 15 years ago that they would be about inner peace and happiness, I would have fallen over laughing! That's the beauty of change. You only have to be open and it comes to you. Fifteen years ago I was miserable and suffering; today I am filled with more love, peace and happiness than I thought possible. Need I say more…?

F I N D H O R N   P R E S S

Life Changing Books

For a complete catalogue,
please contact:

Findhorn Press Ltd
117-121 High Street,
Forres IV36 1AB,
Scotland, UK

t +44 (0)1309 690582
f +44 (0)131 777 2711
e info@findhornpress.com

or consult our catalogue online
(with secure order facility) on
www.findhornpress.com

For information on the Findhorn Foundation:
www.findhorn.org